The Unforgiveness Detox Copy

The Book that will Propel You on Your Healing Journey

Latoya Shea

COPYRIGHT

ABOUT AUTHOR

Being on her own after being homeless at the age of 13, Latoya has experienced and triumphed over many obstacles.

Inspired by the many that has influenced her life, she has lived a life dedicated to service and education. This has led her on a deep spiritual journey and intimacy with God.

She has been known by many titles such as health inspector, veteran, nurse anesthetist, prophet, and teacher until she finally accepted her calling as God's vessel to do good and guide many back to Him as a Spiritual Life Coach.

Her mission is to help ONE BILLION people overcome trauma so that they can live the life that they were created to live.

If you have any questions or need support or guidance, she may be reached at:

coachlatoyashea@gmail.com

www.latoyashea.com.

f facebook.com/latoyashea

instagram.com/coachlatoyashea

CONTENT

ACKNOWLEDGEMENTS

There are so many to thank who have helped me on my journey.

Family: Allen, Bentley, Bunsie, Mykoo, Shea, Stewart, Taylor.

Friends: Asante, BronxCare fam, Chessare, Evans, Glasgow, Grey, Harding, Samuel.

...And most of all, God, without whom there'd be no healing nor journey.

I am grateful for you all.

INTRODUCTION

Like many of my friends and coaching clients, I'm guessing you've opened this book with just one eye open, both fearing the suggestion of the dreaded "F" word (forgiveness) and yet equally aware of the painful cycle of life you're in right now. You're battling with which one you should give your energy to.

It is true that both forgiveness and unforgiveness are hard indeed.

If you're starting to sense that forgiveness is a path you need to walk, whether by your own discovery or a suggestion of a therapist or coach, but you're angry and resentful about it, I get that. For most, forgiving the very people that caused you so much pain feels like pouring salt in a wound, and it doesn't seem fair. It's okay. You're in the right place, and you're allowed to feel that way.

If keeping one eye shut and one foot out the door feels safe for you, I gladly welcome that posture. Furthermore, I honor the other eye that is still choosing to be open and the other foot that you have allowed to step in this direction.

Maybe you have yet to conclude that unforgiveness is the beast that you've been wrestling with, but "something" felt like you should pick this book up; you're also in the right place. I don't believe that's by chance, but rather an inner leading that sometimes works for us when we don't know how to help ourselves.

Wherever you are on the spectrum of forgiving those who hurt you, know that I'm not here to shame you into forgiving and not necessarily even talk you into it. Forgiveness is not something I can convince you to embrace within the pages of this book, but I can give you a foundation of truth for your heart to meditate on. With hurt and trauma, our emotions can bounce around like a ping-pong ball, and it's really easy to lose perspective of what's actually healthy for us.

Anger and vengeance can "feel" empowering short-term but will quickly turn on us like a middle-school clique.

My top goal is to pull the curtain back on the invisible snakes of the soul so that when the swell of emotions seems overwhelming, its source is revealed, and the elimination process can finally begin.

I am here to hold your hand and be a guiding light to help you understand what you've been going through. So very little is talked about unforgiveness and its systemic impact on your entire life: how it happened, what it's been doing to you, and how it's the hidden devil that's been causing so much weight and compounding pain in your life. It keeps you locked up from going after your true life's purpose.

If there's one thing that will empower you to get unstuck, it will be to finally understand the whole truth about where you are in your journey.

There is a fascinating connection between what's going on in our "invisible" souls and our daily lives: anger triggers, failure cycles, self-sabotage, chronic pain, etc.

We spend thousands of dollars on prescription medication and hundreds of hours beating ourselves up for what might be "wrong" with us. The lies that you're bad, evil, crazy, mean, lazy, psycho, and so on have intimidated you into believing you are those things, pushing you further and further into the quicksand.

You're actually a brilliant person, full of unique world-changing ideas and abilities, and I believe you are closer than you think to realizing those dreams: just inches away on the ruler of your life. The career you want, the physical health you're desiring, the relationship you long for, the great idea you'd like to pursue; it's all right there.

If I can at least help you "see" the intermingling of the happenings in your soul and problematic things that continue to arise in your life, then you're free to take your time and tackle those things.

I believe we all have a built-in bottleneck in life, like a beautiful hourglass.

Although it might feel like crushing pressure or being stuck at the moment, the narrowing in the sandglass is made to benefit us.

Imagine the bottom half as your wide-open future, ready to be filled with new and exciting things, but the narrow piece in the middle is very picky about what it allows to pass through. Only the parts of your past that benefits your future can pass through. The sticky, achy, hurtful parts that are yet to be reconciled just accumulate at the bottleneck. And we find ourselves feeling stuck.

The sheer pressure and discomfort of this "mid-life" can't-move-forward state of being cause such a disruption in our lives that we cannot move forward until we are forced to do something about our past...or else. Our destiny is literally putting a demand on us to offload our "junk" so we can be free to fly.

Like I said a few seconds ago, the invisible happenings of the soul are abstract, just like the wind. We can feel their impact, both good and bad, but we can't see them. Unforgiveness works the same way. It is our addiction to our pasts that is stored in our minds, preventing us from moving forward because we have made that our entire story. So what happens to us becomes the verdict of our future; that is a lie!

It presents itself as a version of comfort to the pain we're experiencing, and as soon as we shake hands and agree to dance, the poison goes to work, slowly, slowly, until we're so far in we can't even see it.

Maybe you've heard the quote, "Unforgiveness is like drinking poison yourself and waiting for the other person to die"...as triggering as that may feel, unforgiveness in your soul is like poison to the body.

To understand the process of something abstract like unforgiveness, we will follow the shot of poison; from ingestion to removal: the unforgiveness detox.

The medical world and all things pertaining to our physical body are what I know; I am a Certified Registered Nurse Anesthetist, a.k.a. the person that puts people to sleep for surgery. I studied Psychology, served in the U.S. Army, graduated from Public Health school, was a health inspector, went to nursing school, worked as a nurse, went to more school, and currently work as a CRNA in a hospital in the Bronx, NY.

None of those achievements, however, have credentialed me to write this book. I earned that degree in the school of hard knocks, which cost me more than any degree ever will.

But I'm here, on the other side of rejection, abandonment, loss, abuse, betrayal, multiple rapes, and homelessness. I'm here, to tell the truth, and to help you understand that there is massive freedom and immeasurable peace on this side of trauma and forgiveness.

The feelings common among many who have successfully forgiven abusers in their life are: heavy burdens being lifted, happiness returning, peace renewed, hope for the future restored, giving and receiving love in healthy ways, all relationships improving, advancement in career situations, self-confidence soaring, empowerment to do "hard things," sleeping better, and physical pain and ailments vanishing.

Many I've interviewed say that if they'd known the benefits forgiveness could bring them, they would've pursued it much sooner.

In the next few chapters, we'll follow the path of poison in our physical body to help us understand what's happening in our "soul" body. You'll find the two share an astounding comparison.

-It all starts with something bad, maybe lots of things bad, that we never asked for (and also didn't deserve).

-In an attempt to wash away the bitter taste we were forced to swallow, we take a sweet shot of poison. It often smells and tastes sweet to disguise its lethal ingredients (otherwise, we wouldn't drink it, Duh!).

Soon we realize something is not right. We may not know what, but we need help, fast!

Upon arrival at the hospital, some tests are run to quickly determine whether your blood level is toxic, and without intervention, death is inevitable.

An extended stay in the hospital allows our body to level out under the observation and care of a medical team. We may need comprehensive treatment and some tools for returning home.

-Home is a great place to return to, healed and equipped enough to recognize poison if it's served again and (unfortunately) experienced enough to never drink it again!

Chapter 1

EXCUSE ME; I DIDN'T ORDER THIS

The sun had set a few hours ago, and the orange in the skies exited slowly. An opportunity for the inky blacks of the night to seep in as the warm Jamaican breeze was taken over by the cool, dampening air. It all stayed but a signal that the day was coming to an end.

My eighth-grade barbecue had been a wild performance; a blend of all kinds of emotions and characters, but I had remained on the side of my new, cool classmate through the night. I had soaked up every moment of this fading freedom, observing people all around as they continued to talk, joke, eat and dance. This had truly been the highlight of my entirely secluded life, and before I knew it, the very first social event I had ever attended was coming to an end.

I had hoped that this would last forever, but nothing ever does, right? So I promptly reported to the exact same spot my mom had told me to come to when she was dropping me off. Walking back to the eventual ordinaries of my life, I noticed that a group of the remaining party attendees turned as they began walking down the street.

One.

Two.

Then all of the outdoor party lights suddenly shut off.

The once well-lit meeting spot was now pitch black, revealing the absence of my mom's car headlights that should've been approaching.

I grabbed the edges of my red and white polka dot dress and, out of the corner of my eye, I nervously glanced from side to side, down each direction of the street, to find still no cars in sight.

Standing alone in the dark, in the pin-drop silent streets of Kingston, Jamaica, I watched the crowd advance further down the street.

I had waited 13 long years to hang out with the other, much cooler kids, hoping for some glimpse of social interaction outside my house. Born to a disinterested teen mom, my grandmother was a strictly 'business only' woman when it came to raising me alongside her children, who were a few years older than I. Our weekends were fully booked for cleaning and church, and I'd spend the rest of my free time on the back porch reading books. My grandma said my bed was far a safer alternative to my friends as "it won't lie on you." Yes, grandma, but it also won't talk...sighs.

But tonight was the night—the night I was finally allowed to go to my 8th-grade barbecue. These few good moments of an unheard social interaction were enough to get me excited. My aunt had chosen one of her dresses to lend to me and had helped fix my hair. I'd never worn anything like this before, and she was hyped up to get me ready as she wanted me to have fun.

My mother agreeing to take me out was itself a miracle. She never took me anywhere, and if we did ever appear together in public, I was to act as her little sister so I wouldn't reveal our most hidden family secret.

This was a night full of firsts, and it seemed like everyone was excited for me. Suddenly, I was full of hope that things might just be a little different from now on.

"Wait fi me!" I nervously shouted as I jogged to the back of the crowd disappearing into the night sky.

I was too scared to wait alone in the dark, so I decided to stick with the group and just watch out for my mom as we walked.

A man came alongside me and, appearing concerned, asked me if I was okay. I told him that I was waiting for my mom and that she'd be here any minute; I had stayed towards the back, so I wouldn't miss mommy's beaming lights.

I guess he had noticed that I had grown nervous and impatient. I didn't like staying alone; I'd much rather stay in the herd. It was odd and ironic how I was both invisible and the most different one there.

"Well, I'm actually walking to a friend a few houses down (insert Jamaican accent). They have a phone if you'd like to call her," he suggested.

"Alright. Thanks!" I naively replied.

Upon arriving at this house, I soon discovered there were no phones to call my mom. Loud music and many people, but definitely no phones.

In just a few moments, it became apparent that the best day of my life had betrayed me; sold me out to the darkness of the night. My 13-year sentence in the prison of isolation and disconnection allowed me one night of freedom before it violently shoved me back into a pit of stolen innocence.

My screams for help could not compete with the deafening bass of reggae music. My voice drowned in that house of horror as they each took their turn raping me. Yes, they. Plural, multiple, repetitive rounds of this burning, unending pain.

As predicted, yes, things were about to change. Just not in a way I had hoped for.

SERVED WHAT YOU DIDN'T ORDER

No one plans for horrible things to happen to them. Despite many of us growing up in incredibly dysfunctional homes, as children, we spend hours rehearsing in our imaginations and at play with the wonderful life we expect to have as adults. Barbie dolls and lego sets hoping to craft our little world as those boxes suggest. But life, unlike those toys, doesn't come with an instruction manual, just a thousand pieces scattered on the floor; a thousand humpty dumpties waiting to be put together again.

When life slaps us with something we never saw coming, along with the shock, hurt, anger, shame, and all of the emotions surrounding the incident itself, there comes too, a level of grief when the life we imagined dies in front of our very own eyes.

The religious girl gets pregnant with the "bad boy" and is left a single mother. A career-ending injury devastating your basketball dreams.

A woman you'd planned to build a family with leaves you for another man; you can fill in the blank, but it's all life-altering; at least the life we'd imagined.

In many senses, it's like our brain was pregnant with our dreams—full of hope, possibility, and expectation and then—BAM! A miscarriage of all that we'd wanted life to be. A fire within as you search for someone to blame. A death to yourself when no one is in the crowd; very much a death that requires grieving before we can even forgive.

This would be the first stage of the process and at the risk of lighting the mood a little. It is just like being super excited to eat your favorite meal that you've been craving, that you've driven all the way home, open up the bag, and find out they messed up your order.

For the poison to enter your system, there must first be a point of entry, a bitter dish, a violation, a crack in the walls of our leaking heart.

THE MOST UNFORTUNATE part of unforgiveness is that something terribly painful preceded it. There must have been a violation first if there was a need for healing and forgiveness. Something cuts you, a wound deep to your heart, a scar imprinted on your soul as you come to be known as the broken guy or girl. This could be by the hands of someone else, by your own, or seemingly by the hands of God. Something difficult that you didn't ask for, want, deserve, and definitely weren't prepared for.

Regardless of where it came from, it's all still there; keeping your gaze fixed on the past, unable to hope for the day ahead. A prisoner to pain and a victim of those pendulums that stayed.

Identifying painful experiences within the last 10-15 years isn't hard for most adults. Depending on how recent the wound is, it's probably pretty obvious. It's possible, however, that your present struggles are connected to hurtful childhood events. You may be unaware that you're still hurting and need to work through those things.

If you have an image or scene in your mind that replays from time to time, it's likely your brain's way of signaling a need to heal that memory. A dying last cry before you go into self-defense, blocking your memories, letting them embed.

Do you have recurring dreams about the past or with people from your past? Sleep allows our conscious mind to rest while the subconscious mind releases stuck memories that need resolution.

Is there a story that comes up often during arguments? Alternatively, a person?

For example, "you don't understand how my parents treated me," or "you're just like my mother/father." Maybe something like "my brother always got everything he wanted" or "my parents never taught me anything."

An honest self-reflection of phrases such as these that come from our mouths will indicate what hurts are still carrying on into our present and with whom we still have offenses.

The Invisible Pain

Maybe there was also physical evidence of what you suffered; hopefully, you were treated for that. Honestly, that is the easy part. It is visible to the eye, takes no special training to identify, and carries zero social stigmas about whether or not you need or should receive help.

You're bleeding out; you need help now!

Your arm is broken in half. Straight to the emergency room.

Are you not breathing? CPR is applied without hesitation.

No one is standing around debating about what the gushing blood might mean or if your dangling arm repair will be covered by insurance or not. And, unless someone is totally demented, it's unlikely that you're being mocked, shamed, or ignored when asking for help and getting medical treatment. The eyes are very good at identifying bodily wounds; it is the pain within that most fail to see.

Injuries to the heart, however, are much different. Heart wounds are generally invisible to the naked eye. For that reason, they are rarely recognized, understood even less, and unfortunately left untreated.

Negative emotions are the closest visible sign of invisible hurts, but those expressions aren't often understood. Emotional intelligence has only been a thing since the early 90s.

Emotional intelligence refers to the ability to identify and manage one's own emotions, as well as the emotions of others. Emotional intelligence is generally said to include a few skills: namely emotional awareness, or the ability to identify and name one's own emotions; the ability to harness those emotions and apply them to tasks like thinking and problem solving; and the ability to manage emotions, which includes both regulating one's own emotions when necessary and helping others to do the same.[1]

EMOTIONS. What are they? Where they come from and what to do with them are not part of our primary education, and most families seem to be dysfunctional or blind towards this area of life. It's no surprise, then, that we struggle to properly identify them, let alone communicate them to others in a healthy way.

---

1. https://www.psychologytoday.com/us/basics/emotional- intelligence

Why do you suppose, since both physical injury and emotional injury have existed since the beginning of time, we are exponentially more advanced in the medical treatment of the body and lacking severely in the mental health/emotional arena?

Could it be because emotional pain is invisible and difficult to conceptualize? That's probably one reason.

Could it also be the prideful stigma around the expression of emotion? And more importantly that our expressions of emotions are rarely returned with empathy and understanding but are misinterpreted and perceived as a personal threat to those observing them. "Awww you broke your hand? Get well soon...I hope it gets better." But tell the same people of harassment and negligence and watch them turn a blind eye. The most they would do is compare your grief to another more influential person who went through a hard time. "Oh, look at them; they made it so why can't you?" This only invalidates the pain, contributing nothing to the healing process. Imagine if you went to the doctor with a broken ankle, and instead of covering you up in plaster and finding a cure, they start comparing you to Michael Jordan and how he suffered through much, much bigger injuries. An individual of modern society simply cannot express emotion without provoking a response from another individual. This is a horrible treatment for an unwell person and a punch to agonizing fracture in one's mental health.

For children, it's common for feelings of loneliness, sadness, grief, exhaustion, frustration, or fear to result in crying or whining. It is a child's unregulated "not good" feeling inside with a limited vocabulary that sparks up into their adult life, lighting a fire on their relationships, thought processes, and their overall way of life. Yet often, it is met with annoyance, criticism, discipline, and anger from their parents. Why?

The answer is that their child's emotions are misinterpreted as rebellion, naughtiness, impatience, and disrespect— which all could put parenting abilities in question. No longer is this a child that needs their parent's guidance to navigate disappointment, but a bratty child who is making the parent "look bad" in public.

Another's emotions become so uncomfortable that rather than simply acknowledging the feeling and supporting them through it, we seek to shut it down by any means necessary: punishment, threats, shaming, mocking, screaming back, and withholding affection.

Does any of this feel familiar to you?

There is no magical time from when something terrible happens to us to when we heal; that's certainly dependent on other factors. When our trauma is not one isolated event but an abusive pattern over several months or years, it may be cutting a wound a little at a time until we have a gaping wound that we think is just a normal part of our life and personality.

The distractions of life feel like a relief, teasers of hope that things might get better. The human spirit, especially in children, is designed with great resiliency and hope for a better day. Children forgive and forget quickly and will certainly learn to adapt their emotions to protect themselves from harmful adults.

Children perceive unhealthy behaviors of adults as responses to something they did wrong and adapt to achieve favorable results.

And that happens over, and over, and over. Maybe we hope it will improve with time, or perhaps we don't recognize it.

Aside from not having proper acknowledgment of your wound and the limited understanding of the pain, it's possible that the wrong people surrounded you at the wrong time, and before you could feel the pain or even acknowledge it, someone with no ability to help you came along and made it worse: a "friend," co-worker, or sibling that poured salt right into your wound.

Maybe you can relate to the story in Oz: The Great and Powerful, starring James Franco, Mila Kunis, Rachel Weiss, and Michelle Williams, among many other well-known actors.

If you haven't seen the movie, it's a prequel to our childhood classic, The Wizard of Oz. It explains the story of how the Wizard, Good Witch (Glinda), and Bad Witch (Theodora) all come to exist long before Dorothy drops in fresh off the Kansas twister.

The Wizard (played by Franco), actually named Oz, starts out as a young man in a similar setting as Dorothy in Kansas. As a traveling magician, he earned a living duping people on stage, which became a trick he used on women often.

He was infamous for wooing women and giving them a music box that was "a very special heirloom of his grandmothers" to make them feel special. Then, when they're head over heels and desiring commitment, he sneaks out, moves on to the next girl, and repeats the same song and dance.

Eventually, Oz messes with the wrong girl and finds himself on the run, barely escaping in his hot-air balloon, only to be instantly met with a raging twister. As you guessed, his hot air balloon ends up crashing in the Land of Oz.

He's helped out of a swamp by a beautiful dark-haired woman named Theodora, who concludes that this gentleman is the fulfillment of a long-standing prophecy of a man. A man who falls from the sky, saves their people and becomes the king.

Of course, being the character he is, the Wizard goes along with her hopes and puts on his usual charm with Theodora. She imagines herself becoming his queen, and he carelessly agrees with appeasement. They danced, and she, too, was given a music box.

Holding hands, they nearly skip into the city of Oz together as she dreams of their life together, and he dreams of power and riches.

Fast forward a bit, details sparing. Theodora peers into her crystal ball and finds Oz, sent by her sister, gallivanting with Glinda the Good. However, at the time, Theodora thinks Glinda is the bad witch when it is her own sister Evanora.

Her cunning sister Evanora finds Theodora gazing into the ball, with tears burning into her face, her heart nearly ripped out of her chest, and offers what seems to be sympathy.

"What's the matter, sister?" she asks.

"Do you think she'll be his queen?" Theodora inquires.

"Of course, she'll be his queen —what did you expect? It can't compete with Glinda's charms. No one can."

"Oh, God, sister...it hurts."

"Such is a broken heart...Precious Wizard did that to you."

"Make it stop."

"Do you want me to?"

Theodora's original sadness of seeing the Wizard with Glinda was exacerbated by her sister until she was overcome with humiliation and moved to anger.

If there's one thing humans don't like, it's the wounding of our egos and the embarrassment of being played for a fool, which is where things get ugly——fast.

Chapter 2

SERVED A SWEET SHOT OF POISON

"One bite is all it takes. One bite, and your world will change forever. One bite and your heart will become impenetrable...."

Evanora holds a shiny green apple out to her sister, whose angry heart is burning tears into her cheeks. Evanora moves closer and closer as the temptation to stop the pain becomes stronger and stronger. It was getting unbearable, and she wanted a quick relief.

"One bite, and you and I will finally share the throne." She manipulates the power of the false hope that is still within reach.

"Unless you'd rather see Oz and Glinda there...." The final lunge of mockery toward Theodora, and she snatches the apple from her sister's hand and bites into the apple.

SERVED A SWEET SHOT OF POISON

Instantly, the eyes of Theodora's heart are open to the reality of evil. She could see all those invisible and unimaginable things she never knew. She becomes aware that Evanora is the wicked witch and begins to gasp for air as her heart becomes arrested by darkness.

Falling to the ground as her transformation takes place, Theodora arises as the ugly, green wicked witch we all know.

Even Evanora is shocked by how hideous she has become and offers to cast a spell to turn her back. But Theodora has taken on, both in appearance and in heart, the poisonous result of unforgiveness and responds,

"No, this is who I am now. I want him to see me like this. I want him to know that he was the one who made me this way."

What a tragic mistake; with a heart overcome with grief and a manipulator waiting to take advantage, Theodora became the villain by deception.

And so it goes with a broken heart——a crack in the walls that leave our soul compromised and vulnerable to poison, like a break in the skin becomes open to infection. It's a wound that never goes away; instead, it keeps on reminding us of the incident by causing pain. Those wounds never get a chance to heal. In some instances, we don't even recognize that the wounds and cramps are there, but both hold us captive. Their trails are evident as they proceed to write life in hard and worrying ways. They make us stand back or back out from time and keep us from having lived in a naked and liberating way. So, how do we break through them and move on?

Scan with your camera app to watch the scene from Oz: The Great and Powerful on YouTube. (I do not own the rights to this movie and am not associated with this YouTube Channel)

YOUR EVANORA

The scene mentioned above from Oz: The Great and Powerful shows the unfortunate transformation of Theodora from a beautiful, kind woman to an ugly witch. What this scene doesn't reveal are Evanora's hidden motives to claim the throne for herself.

The arrival of the Wizard, and Theodora's sincere belief that he was a fulfillment of the prophecy, were both dangerous threats to her crown, and she couldn't risk losing her chance. So, not only did she prey on her sister's vulnerability, but she poured the shot of poison and served it with a smile.

An entertaining plot for a movie but hardly amusing when these tragedies unfold in real life.

I wonder who was in your company when you got hurt? Who were the Evanoras that came to "show support" and brought with them a flask of toxic comfort?

A friend, family member, or co-worker? Maybe a support group, social media account, or organization?

What were their motives that led them to so generously make themselves available to be a shoulder to cry on as they poured you a shot of poison?

A common offense? Some misery that needed company? Did they need your angry energy to join their cause? Your money? Your vote? Or they simply had the best intentions while blindly leading the blind.

Presented to you by a smiling, familiar face offering comfort, camaraderie, revenge——relief from the pain. In your desperation, you grabbed that sweet shot to chase the bitterness of despair, and before it hit your stomach, your transformation began.

Was there such a person that served you the poison? A divisive family member, your loyal "best friend"? A lawyer that could solve your problems for a hefty down- payment? Someone who tempted you with solace but delivered you sin? Took advantage of your broken heart and used you to serve their selfish motive?

If there's not a face or name, maybe a club? A gang? A social media account?

A company of misery that shared your pain and fed you poison? A group of individuals that gathered to commiserate and spur on the slow death into victimhood or a quick ride to jail?

Maybe you're being encouraged to smear the one that hurt you on social media, write an article about them, expose them, hurt them, withhold love, power, children, money from them—anything to repay them for the damage they caused you.

But alas, unforgiveness has an appetite for revenge that will never ever be satisfied and, in turn, betrays you in the end. You will be the witch! You will be the joke. You will be the one sitting in a prison cell (physical, mental, or emotional), paying a sum of money you can't afford, or worst: sitting somewhere 10 years later - filled with regrets and unrealized dreams.

So I implore you to dig deep. Who is your Evanoras? Is it you?

A personal reflection takes a bit more bravery than identifying a sneaky witch in a movie, but it will mean everything to your detox. It may even threaten the very people you "think" are your support system. You might initially feel irritated by this suggestion; you may tend to defend and guard "your people."

Stay connected.

Learn positive strategies. You want to make awareness of those places where you put others' interests before your own. This will take a lot of attention and contemplation since learning to stick up for yourself may initially seem really strange to you.

It's very possible that "your people" are not as calculated and intentionally evil as Evanora but rather have a common wound they have yet to heal and are pulling you under.

Think about it. Evaluate whether your support system: friends, confidants, groups, books, clubs, therapists—is leading you down the path to healing. Do you feel positive, happier, healthier, wiser, and more peaceful when you're with them?

Or do you feel greater anger, deeper contempt, or tempted into risky, illegal, or unhealthy behavior? Do you have an opinion and a voice that is heard and respected, or are you steamrolled into doing things you don't want to do?

Just think about it right now, what is in the cup that they're handing you...or that you're handing to yourself?

SOMETHING SWEET TO CHASE IT DOWN?

"Oh, hm. This coffee tastes sweet. You know I don't like sugar in my coffee," Dr. George Blumenschein told his ex-lover as she served him some "special" Columbian coffee at her home in Houston, Texas.

Blumenschein and his co-worker Dr. Ana Maria Gonza- lez-Angulo had been having an affair for almost a year and a half when the news surfaced that he'd been trying to have children with his live-in girlfriend.

After apparently calming down from her initial fit of jealous rage, Ana invited Blumenschein over to reconcile over a sweet cup of coffee.

"Oh, sorry. Yeah, it's Splenda. It's a super expensive blend from Columbia though, so don't waste it."

A vulnerable moment, perhaps. Blumenschein was probably feeling a little guilty for how everything went down. He likely had his guard down; even if the sweet coffee was signaling a red flag, he certainly was not willing to offend Ana anymore, so he proceeded past the warning signs and drank the whole thing.

It would be a matter of hours before his vision became blurred, and his heart started racing. For a normally healthy guy, it wasn't hard to notice that his health was quickly spiraling downward.

It wouldn't be long before it was discovered that the sweet coffee he'd stomached earlier that morning was spiked with ethylene glycol, a sweet substance found in antifreeze. Gonzalez had not been trying to smooth things over but instead was trying to kill him.

Because he acted quickly, he received urgent care and was put on emergency dialysis to help filter the toxins from his body. He did not die but lives today with only 40% function of his kidneys. His life may be shortened, or at the very least, he'll need a kidney transplant in the future. [1]

UNFORGIVENESS IS a Sweet Poison

---

1. https://www.usatoday.com/story/news/nation/2014/09/29/cancer- doctor-poisoned-coffee/16436557/

Chapter 3

SOMEONE, PLEASE CALL 911

"Oh my gosh, I can't breathe again! Wake up, I can't breathe!"

Liz cracked her eyes open to see her husband James sitting on the edge of the bed with both hands over his chest. As she blinked to straighten out the sticky, dry contact lenses left in her eyes, she noticed his face dressed with the same panicked expression she'd seen almost every day for almost the last six weeks. Actually, on and off much of the 8 years they'd been married.

"Liz, I can't breathe. My side hurts right here. Feel it!" he cried as he grabbed her hand and placed it over the same area he'd always indicated on the left side of his chest.

As usual, she felt nothing.

Liz did her best to calmly appease his frantic questions, although underneath, she was becoming a bit annoyed. Her husband's constant paranoia that each ache and pain he felt might be instantly killing him was getting old. It was an odd phenomenon to see the person in front of her, clearly, physically okay, proven by at least 15 physicians to be healthy, yet so convinced that death was imminent.

"Go get the inhaler. Do you think I should go back to the ER?"

"No, you don't need to go there. They can't do anything else for you."

He had gone to the local emergency room 3 times in the past week by ambulance, returning with no other diagnosis than the one he continually rejected—anxiety disorder.

Please, dear God, we have no insurance, and we're racking up ER AND ambulance ride bills for NOTHING, she thought.

Walking to the hallway closet to find whatever concoction of Xanax, albuterol, and Motrin she could find, she heard him talking on the phone a few rooms down. "Yes, I live at 222 Westway Drive. I can't breathe. I'm just really not feeling good."

He'd called 911. Again.

Ahhhh. Liz felt so helpless in those moments. She knew after multiple blood draws, CT scans, and EKGs done at various hospitals across the nation, wherever they happened to live or be traveling at the time, his health was cleared. Yet chronic pain and panic attacks that seemed to be ambushing him multiple times per day now had him completely paralyzed from living a normal life.

This was around the time I met James.

James grew up in a violent home that billowed a negative atmosphere. He was often demeaned and told by his parents that he was "so stupid". His parents introduced him in public as "James with a learning disability" to pre-excuse any negative behavior that one might observe during their time of interaction.

The earliest beatings James could remember started when he was 4 years old. He was parented through shame; anything he did "wrong" or "annoying" received severe criticism until he was reduced to a bad kid. At 7, he was thrown through a glass table because his father was annoyed by him. He was always saying sorry for making any mistakes. He didn't want to be beaten.

Beatings sometimes happened with a metal dog leash or shoes being hurled across the room at him. He told me he couldn't recall a day in his life when he didn't cry or have bruises put on him.

He was the first kid to get kicked out of the catholic school right by his house because he hit a nun for hitting him. His grandfather told him to defend himself, so he thought he had to defend himself from the nun who was beating him across his face.

In the neighborhood, this created a black sheep label around James. Because of these labels, he never felt assured or as if he was good enough.

James was then shipped to the public school system and put in the special education system because James would get in fights. It wasn't because he couldn't do regular school work; it was because he was in a school where he had to defend himself. So he was the first in his neighborhood to be suspended for fighting.

In the 7th grade, James was thrown out of an entire school system for getting in a fight and always getting in trouble. He had a problem with authority. No one ever assumed he was acting out because of the hurt he felt from being abused at home.

Outside the home, James excelled in sports. He started to garner a local reputation that he was good enough to play with kids four years older than him. Still, his sister would always spread rumors about him to get him kicked off the team and abused by his parents or older kids; she hated anything James excelled at.

Because of athleticism, James started receiving constant attention from girls, something he wasn't used to. They made him feel good about himself.

Once he turned 18, he was strong enough to fight back. They stopped hitting him but worked fervently to control his behavior with shameful and demeaning talk.

As an adult, James realized he had to deal with his trauma.

Should parents use force to raise their children? They certainly should not. Violence of any kind from anyone is unacceptable, but it is especially so when its server is the very people charged with the nurturing and well-being of a person. Indeed, why should we resort to violence when there are less harmful ways of resolution? Parental violence has been found to increase with the accompanying rise in the cost of living and the increase in violence worldwide. Parents are exposed to more traumatic events (directly and/or indirectly) whilst being forced to work longer hours to maintain their family's livelihood. Does this make it acceptable? Absolutely not! But it certainly holds true to the adage “It takes a village to raise a child,” and this includes the welfare of parents as well.

Abuse of any kind destroys the lives of children...who, in turn, become adults with 'childhood issues'. It shatters their self-esteem, morals, hope, and joy; and robs them of their innocence.

THIS IS a true story from a coaching client of mine. When he came to me, his life was riddled with panic attacks and chronic pain. On top of those physical experiences, he was really stuck in life. His life had been hovering in the same cycle for the past few years without breaking through. His marriage was strained, finances were constantly under pressure, and most relationships were short-term. He wasn't active, mainly paralyzed on the couch whenever he could be.

While physical manifestations of unforgiveness are common, they aren't always present. Across the board, one thing is common in all of my clients who are carrying unforgiveness, and that is the feeling of being stuck, which is usually manifested in their professional careers, marriage, parenting, motivation, or spiritual life. Their body, soul, spirit, and relationships have gotten as far as they could with their current weight, and are now saying, "NOPE. WE CAN'T GO ANY FURTHER. WE CAN NOT TAKE OFF AND FLY WITH THIS MUCH BAGGAGE."

The mind, body, and soul connection is so strong. When one is experiencing pain, all of them do! Although I (obviously) fully support the world of medicine, it does have limitations when it comes to healing chronic issues stemming from some type of trauma.

Medical doctors have the ability to assess tangible, physical symptoms with tests: blood draws, X- rays, CT scans, and vital signs. Often the physical diagnosis is matched with a physical solution. Many of those medications often help the individual experience less of the undesired symptoms, yet the root of the issue remains stained in the mind and soul of the person, seeking to manifest itself in some other form. With the latest, the medical world is still very limited in how we can identify and treat the invisible wounds of the soul that manifest in the physical body.

Much of the population, like in my client's case at the beginning of the chapter, would prefer to have a pill to fix a physical problem than to even entertain the idea that something is mentally or emotionally "wrong" with them. And that's a major contributor to what keeps the pockets of pharmaceutical companies full. Again, not opposed to medication at all when needed, but it has become a "microwave" solution to fixing deep emotional hurt and trauma. Much of the American population remains blissfully ignorant to the invisible traumas rearing their ugly heads right in the middle of our professional lives.

Although "mental illness" still carries a level of shame and embarrassment, it's easier still to admit a physical diagnosis like a "chemical imbalance" rather than "depression caused by severe exposure to abuse and trauma". Especially for professionals or people who feel like they should be "normal"---those that got really good at learning what "socially acceptable" behavior is and have worked so hard to put on brave "professional" faces.

Trauma is defined as an event that causes severe physical or mental pain. It is a severe torment to the body and disrupts its natural equilibrium. It is defined as an emotional wound that causes psychological harm. Shock and denial are common reactions immediately following an event. Long-term effects include erratic emotions, flashbacks, and strained relationships. There are many different types of trauma that can affect an adolescent, and without proper treatment for the traumatic event, the adolescent may struggle to adapt and develop into adulthood.

Its impact can be catastrophic at times, causing harm to both one's self and one's social identity. Genocide, objectification of others, death, atrocities, and haunting are all conditions that strongly impact the senses. The consequences of these incidents are traumatic.

Adults who have experienced or are experiencing the effects of trauma may exhibit symptoms such as difficulty starting new tasks, blame, guilt, concern for safety, depression, inability to trust (especially those in power), fear of taking risks, disturbed sleep, eroded self-esteem/confidence, inability to concentrate, or panic attacks.

Some people have no symptoms, while others have Post-traumatic Stress Disorder (PTSD), characterized by flashbacks, avoidance, numbing of responsiveness (including substance abuse), the persistent expectation of danger, constriction (dissociation, zoning out), and memory impairment.

I'd say this is especially difficult for men or "alpha" type women who struggle to explore the uncertainty of vulnerability. Many just learned how to "pull up their bootstraps and get to work" and created successful careers for themselves by simply hiding their hurt with more work and their natural abilities. Their business might have million-dollar revenue, but family life is painful and disastrous, and their ability to find balance in life is nonexistent.

Unresolved trauma, along with unforgiveness, will find its breaking point somewhere. It's like a giant ship that hits an iceberg.

Each ship, or person, might collide with a different iceberg: financial, marriage, parenting, business or professional career, legal trouble, mental health, physical illness—which has put holes in our ship.

Our ships might stay afloat for a while; we may be able to stay afloat and convince other people to hop on board, "everything is fine" for a while, but sooner or later, the small hole becomes larger and larger, and water comes rushing in faster and faster. People aboard our ship begin realizing we are no longer "safe," and if they aren't committed to helping us, begin to bail as fast as they can. And to be honest, who can blame them? We each have small buckets, and what can those do for an entire ship that's halfway underwater?

I've created an assessment to help you gauge where you are on your healing journey. Click here to get started...can't wait to hear if you're a yacht, canoe, or sail boat :).

Chapter 4

THE INTERVENTION

"You've got to be f*ckin kidding me," was the only response Sharon could angrily mutter when her therapist suggested that her triggers of anger would improve once she forgave her abusers.

Sharon had been in therapy since she was 17. She was molested almost nightly since the age of 3 by her much older brother. On top of the constant abuse from her brother, she had to deal with her mother. When she finally told her, she brushed it off and turned the suspicion back on Sharon, snidely muttering, "You were probably asking for it." Clearly, her mother was a very unkind woman, among other adjectives.

Sharon had endured so much intense childhood trauma in those formative years that by her late teens, she'd begun "switching" into different personalities, and, at one point, she displayed 12 different identities with separate names, voices, facial expressions, and body language.

By the age of 50, she'd been through virtually every form of therapy on the planet and had been prescribed countless colorful cocktails of anti-psychotic pills. Her entire adult life had been spent trying to integrate all of her personalities back into one identity.

Dealing with her triggers of anger was becoming increasingly problematic, however. To Sharon, they were random outbursts, appearing out of nowhere over things that were no big deal to most. These 'unexplainable' outbursts began causing a great deal of strain in her relationships, as shared with her therapist, which prompted the suggestion that Sharon begins to forgive her brother, mother, and every abuser and enabler that contributed to her childhood nightmare.

Dissociative Identity Disorder (DID), formerly known as Multiple Personality Disorder, is a disorder in which two or more distinct identities alternately control a person's consciousness and behavior. If the altered personalities are not identified and treated in the early stages of development, they may begin to fight for control of the body. This could happen because the alternate personalities have become an equal part of the person, and no alternate can always be in control. Although DID is more commonly diagnosed in late adolescence and early adulthood, most diagnoses occur 5-10 years after the onset of symptoms. Furthermore, DID appears to be more common in females, those who have a close relative with DID, and generally occurs during the developmentally sensitive stages of childhood.

"I was pissed. I'd spent so many years undoing the damage that they caused. Thousands of my own dollars I'd spent to just be "normal," and now I have to do more? What a cruel joke."

Her sentiments aren't uncommon; forgiving is one more thing to do when healing from traumatic events and often is the last chapter in a very long story.

It feels like you're letting them off the hook. Like what they did to you is okay, but it really is not. It's releasing yourself from the weight that connects you to them. It's the best thing I could've done; if I'd known how much lighter and happier I would have felt, I would've done it much sooner. There is a new freedom that comes when you've revoked your abuser's rights to your future.

When you haven't forgiven, your soul is tied to the abuser in the past, connected by a huge weight. Your soul continually stays focused on what was done to you, and whatever we focus on is magnified. So a minor infraction from another person, even a misunderstood joke, would be perceived as a continuation of abuse that was continuing in your soul. Your emotional filter was totally broken, and your nervous system was always supportive of that.

Blumenstein, our poisoned doctor from chapter two, required outside intervention to filter the toxins from his blood.

On a graph, most people imagine healing as a straight line rising upward, indicating progress. Despite the fact that they recognize that healing has ups and downs, they still expect the movement to average out to a straight-line indicating improvement. When they think of progress in this way, they consider returning to a familiar issue they believe they have already dealt with as backsliding and feel as if they are starting over.

However, I prefer the concept of "recursion," which I believe more accurately describes what people go through when they are healing. The term "recursion" comes from computer science and refers to a programming method in which the ultimate solution to a problem is dependent on previous aspects of that problem being solved. Consider a spiral staircase to best explain the recursive process. Instead of a straight line, what you see is a circular line that rises from one level to the next. When you walk up a spiral staircase to a higher level and look out the window, the view is the same as it was at the same point on the lower level, but your perspective has shifted.

This, I believe, describes how we recover from emotional traumas, losses, and suffering in our lives. We keep coming back to the same problem. Although this appears to be regression (going backward) when represented as a straight line, when represented as a spiral, we can see we are moving upwards and dealing with the same issue, albeit in a different way.

Many people associate forgiveness with letting go or moving on. True forgiveness, however, goes a step further, offering something positive—empathy, compassion, understanding—to the person who has hurt you. Because of this, forgiveness is both a virtue and a powerful construct in positive psychology. Outside of scientific circles, however, many people are perplexed by the concept.

One common but mistaken belief is that forgiveness means absolving the person who has hurt you. However, forgiveness is not synonymous with justice, nor does it necessitate reconciliation. A former victim of abuse should not reconcile with an abuser who is still potentially dangerous. However, the victim can still develop empathy and understanding.

But what is forgiveness anyway? From the Latin 'perdonare', to forgive means to give completely without reservations. Keywords "without reservation." What exactly are we giving? Well, everything that we were not born with. Everything that is foreign to our souls and body. That is the purpose of all those painful emotions and ruminating thoughts. They serve as our soul's immune system to let us know that, hey, something that is undesirable has infiltrated our being. And the more we ignore it, the stronger it gets. So rather than putting a band-aid of alcoholism, drugs, workaholism, overeating – or whatever your chosen addiction might be – just kick the toxin to the curb once and for all and be over with it.

Allow me to throw you back to high school anatomy and physiology for just a moment to remind you what our kidneys are designed to do in a healthy body.

OUR BODY'S FILTRATION SYSTEM

The kidneys actually have several functions, but our focus, for now, is the critical job of filtering our blood.

Blood enters the kidneys, and they either add or remove contents (including toxic substances) depending on the body's needs. The filtered blood exits the kidneys and goes on to other vital organs, while the toxins and waste is sent to our bladder to be eliminated from the body during urination.

This process is totally involuntary, meaning we never have to think or take conscious action for our kidneys to function; we're just built that way; it happens for us, 24/7, without a single decision having to be made. With all the mild contaminants we ingest daily, the kidneys do a remarkable job at flushing our system clean.

FILTRATION SYSTEM ON POISON

In the case of poison ingestion, physical symptoms and lab tests performed in the emergency room would indicate the presence of harmful substances in the bloodstream.

While the kidneys normally filter out the everyday, minor toxins, they cannot filter quickly enough the concentrated load of toxins in the bloodstream after drinking poison. For a body to survive such a dose of poison, it needs an external intervention and filtration. If the poison is still present in the stomach, the contents would be evacuated in a very uncomfortable procedure of "pumping the stomach." Although the body quickly goes to work digesting whatever we take in, any amount that can be prevented from passing into the digestive system and bloodstream is helpful in preventing blood toxicity. The kidneys cannot filter a concentrated load of poison. If caught in time, the kidneys can get some assistance from a machine called dialysis.

Dialysis involves two IV needles placed in a patient's arm and connected to a blood filtration machine. One IV sends blood from the body to the machine, and the other IV receives the filtered blood back into the body. For the time being, the body's filter, or the gatekeeper of our body, must be bypassed, and an external method must be used for the patient's survival. In essence, our natural filtration system is out of order.

OUR SOUL'S FILTRATION SYSTEM

Our soul's filtration system under 'normal' circumstances is a bit trickier because we all come from different childhoods and experiences, with different events being traumatic from one person to the next.

Since children, in almost every sense, are like a blank slate, we'll use a child growing up in a healthy home. They are pure and innocent. They believe you when you say you'll do something and hold you accountable until you do. They also are incredibly forgiving, possessing an impressive ability to show mercy and move on.

I believe we are all designed with this blank slate, and from the moment of conception, other people begin writing on it. Some good stuff and some bad.

For most of our years, things have been happening all around us, and unfavorable things could be happening to us often. In an ideal situation, we take in those circumstances, mentally and emotionally process them to the best of our abilities, and then we make a decision about what's going to happen in our hearts next. This could happen multiple times per day or week based on our surroundings. Ideally, a child gets hurt or offended; some time passes, they have an opportunity to forgive, they choose to move on, and all is right in the world again. Much like our body's urinary system, we take in external emotional events, process good vs. bad, keep the good, and let go of the bad.

OUR SOUL ON POISON

To look at how our soul gets poisoned, we'll set aside major traumatic events that may have been held on to for years and look at a micro version of this process.

I'm sure you've had one of those days, just like we all do, where it starts off totally wrong. Your dog poops next to your bed, you step in it when you wake up, fall down, hit your head, you're late to work because you had to disinfect your body and floor, traffic was bumper to bumper, you spilled your coffee in your car as you peeled around the corner, and you arrive at work only to find out a project is running behind. PAUSE.

None of the circumstances are fun, but if one didn't so quickly impact the other, we'd have time to get mad, vent a little, realize everything will be okay, and we'd soon recover from the inconvenience. The event would be ingested, filtered, and released. This is our healthy filtration system.

However, on the days that don't provide time to process and release, where one domino crashes against the next, the "toxins" just build up, and our "filter" becomes overloaded. Our system starts to become toxic, and cannot handle the overwhelm of incoming bad news. UNPAUSE.

Your kind co-worker approaches you to let you know that she's so sorry, but your project is going to be delayed another day. Normally, not a big deal, but your system has reached its capacity, and Cathy co-worker is about to get covered with a verbal explosion of toxic frustration. Your filter has been totally disabled, and Karen is now the object of your emotional vomit. She stands frozen as the poison bubbles out all over her, as you blame her for never being on time, stressing you out, and you're unsure if she is even fit to work there. Exhale. Hm. You actually feel a little better now that you've released all that stress, and your system starts to normalize.

Until you see Karen's sweet eyes fight back the tears that have already snuck down her beet-red face, a toxic transfer has taken place—-from one person to the next. It didn't get flushed down the toilet, just passed from one person to the next.

This is a micro example, or we'd call it an "acute" injury in the hospital. A sudden sickness or injury occurred. Stretched out over the years and slowly building up in our systems would be called a "chronic" injury or illness.

Imagine the toll it takes on our bodies and souls to carry unrecognized toxins inside us for years and years? It's no wonder pharmaceutical companies are making billions of dollars. Who could possibly bear the emotional burdens of prolonged poison?

Much like the physical symptoms that indicate our bodies have been poisoned, there are emotional signs that signal the presence of unforgiveness.

Anxiety, depression, anger, bitterness, contempt, insecurity, shame, confusion, avoidance, and hopelessness, to name a few. The variety depends on who you're holding accountable in your heart: yourself, another person, or God.

It's not often that individuals are able to recognize the root of these emotions on their own, but rather when they are reflected back by another person or someone who recognizes it and verbalizes it. Our normal "filtration system" has been damaged and needs outside help to even notice what's happening.

Displaying extreme anger toward a spouse for a minor infraction probably indicates a festering wound that hasn't been resolved, a much deeper issue that needs discussion and forgiveness.

Feeling like a victim and always acting like people are "doing you wrong" and "treating you bad" could also be a sign that you haven't forgiven someone who has done something to you, and you've remained yoked to that scenario, focused on it, and it has infiltrated your entire belief system.

If you have one solid person in your life that knows you, loves you, and will tell you the truth, consider yourself very lucky. They are your "external filter" and will likely let you know when you're 'off.'

There are times in our lives when the people around us don't embody those elements. In that case, a therapist or a spiritual coach is a really great idea. If you have unresolved trauma and anger, your ability to clearly 'see' and your ability to filter out poison has been compromised, which is now left circulating through your body.

Does everyone need outside help? No! There are those who have worked to become self-aware and can recognize when offenses come and have developed good habits of dealing with those offenses quickly so as not to accumulate poison in their system. If we learn to become familiar with the happenings in our hearts, we can deal with them quickly and potentially on our own.

When a child has a toxic parent, several forgiveness issues arise, resulting in an abnormal "attachment" to the parent that interferes with the need for protection. "I don't understand it," many people with toxic parents say. I know my parent continues to hurt me and is unconcerned about my needs, but I feel obligated to be there for her because I am afraid of losing her." Understanding this attachment allows you to move more easily through the process of forgiveness and protect yourself from the parent and other similar people.

There is a fear of abandonment: Part of the problem is that the fear of abandonment outweighs the fear of being hurt by the parent. This is frequently the result of childhood neglect, abandonment, or the threat of abandonment. It hurts the child more to believe "My parent doesn't love me," which translates to "I'm not lovable," than to believe "She's right—I'm bad." "I need to improve." As a result, some people continue to hold on to the attachment even if it means viewing themselves negatively rather than accepting that the parent is incapable of genuine and unconditional love. It's natural for a child to believe that "if my own parent can't love me, I must not be lovable," but an adult can challenge that belief and recognize that the failure is in the parent, not the child.

Unfortunately, for most of my clients and people that I have helped throughout the years, it is never so black and white. Most cases of neglect and inability to express love stem from generations of hurt.

Still, it is necessary to mourn the loss of the parental "image." Another aspect of attachment is that it is not always to the parent but to the parent's "image." There are so many people who have been abused or neglected by their parents or guardian and believe they have grieved and forgiven the parent. The issue is that they haven't often grieved their true loss: that their parent will never be the parent they want or deserve (their "image" of the parent). They are in denial about their loss, so they continue in the same pattern with the parent, hoping for and attempting to create the relationship they desire, which may never exist.

Before we continue though, I think that this is as good a time as any to note that mourning them does not mean that you hate them or cease to love them. It simply means that you unburden them and yourself from your expectations. And you then learn to love them as they are for who they are. While this is by no means easy, it is necessary.

Notice that this entire time we've been focusing on your response? Good! That is because forgiveness and healing does not have to include the perpetrator. Healing does not always have to involve the parent or anyone else, for that matter. If they are in a space where they can accept their role in the incident(s), then they can be helpful in the process. However, this is not always the case, especially with toxic relationships. As a result, healing does not always involve the transgressor. In fact, in some cases, it is preferable not to involve the toxic person because they are more likely to obstruct rather than help the process.

However, one reason to heal before the parent's death (if possible) is that having a different kind of relationship with that parent can empower you. But honestly, for the sake of transparency, my belief is that you should love and forgive EVERYONE. But for those of you that may disagree or struggle with this notion, the empowerment bit might be a great motivator. For example, if you refuse to accept criticism, if you can confront the parent's behavior, if you can see yourself as separate from the parent and value yourself regardless of how your parent treats you, you will feel more powerful and confident in yourself. And not just in that particular relationship, but in all relationships.

That opportunity, however, is not always available, but healing is. Healing is ultimately within each of us. But be patient with the process and recognize that you may address the issues at different levels until you realize you are no longer reacting in the old ways and that you have healed.

Chapter 5

EXTENDED STAY

"It's been one whole year," Betsy posted on the anniversary of the finalization of her divorce.

Watching Betsy process a very public downfall of her marriage was truly an experience of beauty from ashes.

Betsy doesn't seem like someone that would be getting divorced. For one, she is around the age when people are getting married, not divorced. She is beautiful, happy, kind, successful, and fun-loving; it all seems so out of place. Maybe that contributed to her shock when she discovered her husband was living a double life with another very young woman who was also married with several children.

Having fairly conservative values, Betsy discovered a massive amount of betrayal had been going on for quite a while; cocaine, strip clubs, and marital money being sent to the other woman. It was a lot.

Articles were being written about this scandal on Reddit as each respective party's friends and followers took sides and hurled angry insults.

Betsy is a classy individual, especially given her age and circumstances, and never took part in the public hate. She did share some vague details about her healing and season of life but never used names, attacked, blamed, or showed signs of vengeance.

She quickly found a life coach and began unraveling the shock wave that'd hit her. Betsy's healing was digesting what happened, where it went wrong, and how deep this mess was.

Divorce papers were served, but she kept her wedding band on. She'd taken her wedding vows seriously and was willing to participate in working through the mess.

After understanding that her husband was not going to be working on their marriage, but in fact, leaving her for the other woman, Betsy was able to begin the process of grieving.

Grieving is the stage that many people brush over.

Finally, on the date the divorce papers were signed, she removed her wedding ring and put it in a drawer.

The initial part of Betsy's healing was digesting what happened, where it went wrong, and how deep of a 'mess' it was.

In the Forgiveness Ward, it's common for folks to stay around for a bit. Now that 'here's' stable and resting, let's talk about what just happened. Now is about the time, after your stomach has been pumped, nurses have stopped rushing, stopped yelling for more supplies—the violent night is over, and you've survived. Your eyes flutter open to the remnant soreness from the previous violent night is totally submitted to the sweetness of relief. Our body rests soundly to the steady beep, beep, and beep of stable vital signs. The sun peers in from cracked window shades, and you feel its warmth.

The doctor leans in the doorway of your room and pulls on the chair next to your bed.

Hey, you.

So...what happened?

That's where I get to pick up. This is where I sit with you, at the edge of your bed, physically or virtually. As a friend and someone who has been used, abused, rejected, unloved, and betrayed also.

AHHHHH....I don't know. I never saw it coming. I just didn't expect it. At all. I was fine one minute, and then the next, I wasn't.

There's no doubt we've all been mistreated by some human being at some point in our life. The rude person at the drive-thru, irritated partner, or a best friend who gossiped about you behind your back; if we've lived in this world full of other humans, it's just inevitable.

It's interesting though, isn't it? Why some of these hurts are easily forgiven—brushed off, forgotten almost instantly, and others burn deep for weeks, months, and sometimes years?

WHY IS THAT? What violations constitute longer periods of healing and forgiveness?

It certainly seems obvious that rude cashiers pale in comparison to a stepfather who molested you or a mother who abandoned you.

The answer is found at the heart level. How close were they? How deep of a need did we have for them?

Critical were they to our own sense of self, success, and happiness?

Was your mother so disconnected while raising you that she never taught you the skills that you needed to successfully navigate womanhood? Motherhood? Wifehood? And now, you're being criticized by a spouse for that lack?

When that criticism comes, our response will likely fall on a spectrum of a few things:

1. Our level of acknowledgment that we both needed wanted and deserved some life-preparation training from our mothers.

2. Our level of forgiving them for not being what we needed at the moment of occurrence.

3. The grace we hold for ourselves (although I believe this is directly proportional to #2)

4. Our ability to have taken personal ownership of how to learn and acquire what was not given to us.

EXPECTATIONS OF RECOVERY from physical heart surgery are much more intensive than a scratch on the hand. Also, what would it look like if someone punched us in the chest a few days after we'd just had heart surgery?

RATHER: We assume the poisoned doctor was relatively healthy at the time of poison ingestion. There was no indication that he was suffering from any illness or disease. But what if he had been? What if he'd already had small doses of poison previously? What if his kidneys were already compromised? If he was on chemotherapy or in a state of very vulnerable health already? Might he have died before even arriving at the hospital?

IN THE SAME WAY, a hurting soul, already holding unforgiveness in their heart, with an already compromised ability to "filter" toxins, is much more susceptible to death, or long-term damage, by toxic unforgiveness.

-WHAT UNHEALED wounds did we have previously that left us vulnerable?

-What beliefs do we have about forgiveness and how it affects our own lives?

-How?

WE ARE ALL INHERENTLY deserving to be deeply loved, attended to, noticed, cared for, comforted, guided, taught, protected, and defended. Now, those lines somehow begin to get foggy once we hurt others—their unforgiveness might begin to categorize us, whether subconsciously or not, as less "worthy" of anything good— including love and forgiveness.

TO BETTER DIGEST the thought of forgiveness, let's take a look at Brian. He is:

-extra-hard working

-positive

-loyal

-chivalrous

-takes good care of himself

-ambitious

A VERY ATTRACTIVE PERSON. He makes good money and enjoys lots of fun activities, but when it comes to finding a mate, he complains he can't ever find a good one; he 'always attracts the bad ones', and date after date just falls apart.

Imagine ONE DAY you happen to overhear your friend on a lunch date. She is telling the suitor across the table about her high school boyfriend, who she'd dated 15 years ago. They were the prom king and queen and planning to get married. However, she'd soon discover that her boyfriend was cheating on her with her best friend, a betrayal that's painful for any person to experience. A legitimate bad deal, no doubt. Her words are still seasoned with resentment and suggestive of how "guys can be such jerks."

NOW, assuming the person across the table has no unhealed emotional trauma that causes him to be attracted to negative and demeaning people or a toxic will to "prove he's different," —- we can probably assume it is off-putting to be told that your gender, whether male or female, "can be such jerks"...

ADDITIONALLY, someone with ambition certainly would be putting up red flags. For a first date, the retelling of a 15-year-old betrayal with the same bitter sting as if it happened yesterday probably indicates that this person isn't ready to "move forward" with new dreams and visions for a new relationship. Some basic "laws of attraction" tell us that someone who is bitterly gripped by past hurts has now clouded her judgment of all men and categorized them as "jerks."

It's become commonplace to say that truly loving another person requires first loving oneself. But how well-founded is this maxim? Is it backed up by scientific or academic research? Is it simply folk wisdom—or perhaps pseudo-wisdom? I've looked for many authoritative studies on this fascinating subject... and found nothing.

I could be wrong, but it always struck me as one of those aphorisms that are accepted as true primarily because it sounds true. And the truism exudes a wise, loving self-compassion. It appears logical that we can't truly know love until we experience it from within—for ourselves. But isn't all of this beggaring the question?

Empirical evidence has led me to a different conclusion about self-love. To me, it's extremely unlikely that a person can be happy unless they can love themselves. That is, healthy self-love and acceptance are both necessary and sufficient—not for loving another, but for a state of inner contentment and well-being. It stands to reason that if you're not on good terms with yourself, you're not going to be happy with life in general.

Again, for the sake of transparency, I should express that even greater than self-love, stands another which no amount of explanation could do justice, nor could all the books in the world begin to contain. And this is the love of God. And no, this isn't some religious mumbo jumbo. And no, I'm not about to go on some rant about it. But I will say that with all the abuses and hurts and heartbreaks and disappointments...then forgiving and healing and overcoming, there is NOTHING that could compare to his agape love. This is the thing that people rave about in their encounters with me. This is the "secret sauce" that they keep asking me for. Only, it's no secret. It's simply the unconditional, unadulterated love of God.

Ok, now that we've established that, let's continue. There are several multi-millionaires in this world who are clearly unhappy. So, there's nothing inherently happy about wealth (and all the luxuries it can buy). Neither can the most fulfilling relationships—even if you are loved, or even adored, by an admiring (and admirable) partner. Because, in the end, your happiness is dependent on your ability to be happy with yourself.

Almost all of us have heard of people who, despite having "it all," end up committing suicide. Despite their apparent success, they believe their entire lives are a charade, that they are essentially frauds—and that one day they will be "found out" and shunned as the imposters they are. Essentially, they despise themselves, harboring a profoundly negative sense of self that clearly outweighs their otherwise impressive life "vita."

Almost all of these individuals' upbringings were marked by non-loving parental abuse or neglect. These experiences, unfortunately, left them with serious doubts about their attractiveness, competence, or basic human worth. They couldn't internalize their later-day accomplishments because they never took advantage of the opportunity to receive longer-term therapy (likely because they didn't believe they could be helped). As a result, their negative, outdated beliefs about themselves continued to undermine, if not completely negate, the many positive things they'd accomplished since childhood.

Furthermore, and in stark contrast to the subject's familiar adage, these same people may have been unquestionably loving toward their spouses and children. So it's difficult to find compelling evidence to support the idea that loving oneself is a prerequisite for loving anyone else. For example, I've seen many people who were capable of caring deeply for others but struggled mightily to extend the same care to themselves. They'd frequently express profound doubts about who they thought they were.

THE PROBLEM WOULD BECOME PRETTY clear to someone with a fair amount of discernment and emotional intelligence— She has not become a "magnet" for her ideal mate but rather a deterrent. Her inability to forgive her boyfriend and best friend from 15 years ago has kept her stuck to the past; weighed down with her head turned backward and focused on the past. It's not pretty obvious why she's spinning circles or feeling "stuck," and because it has spanned a 15-year timeline, she's become completely blind to her patterns.

AS A GOOD FRIEND, you recognize that the high school betrayal WAS very painful. You also know that your friend wants to get married to a great guy and literally has no idea what her problem is. She fears that she is unlovable, not beautiful, or successful enough— unworthy of love. And that is the story that she believes. Rather than having the ability to recognize that the betrayal was not her fault in any way, she forgives, heals, and sees herself as someone worthy of the love that she simply hadn't found it yet at 17. True for most people.

It is true what they say, "As a man thinketh in his heart, so is he." Unfortunately, many think of that little organ pumping in our chest upon hearing it. But in the original Hebrew, in which the Proverb was written, it translates to soul, NOT heart. And since we know that the soul is the mind, will, and emotions, then we know that a man is as he thinks, feels, and desires. Which is another spin on the good old "Ask and it shall be given you"...

SHE'S ASKING for your help. The problem is obvious. She's come to a crossroads and has a choice to make.

Without a great friend who could help her see the truth of the issue, she may spend thousands of dollars, vulnerable at the hands of fear-mongering sales ploys, and begin investing her money and years of time into Botox, to make herself more attractive—OR— she could begin to isolate herself, retracting from the pain of rejection, OR be left vulnerable and settle for a guy who earns a lot of money but treats her like the person she has told herself she is—- unloved, and unworthy.

Do you see the mass misfortune of what's happening here?

The devastating scenarios that unfold and play out over not having someone to help us see the truth and to work towards forgiveness and releasing of hurt?

AND IT HAPPENS over and over and over. Traumas and hurt are happening every second, and without the intervention of forgiveness, we begin forming narratives and misguided half-truths. How wounded people wounded us, as we took the bait and believed it all. It took two people. Two men, each with their own wounds and vulnerabilities, totally disqualify her from a beautiful marriage.

AGAIN, wanting to be the friend who tells you the truth

—- we can apply literally any "stuck person" life here. Something happened. Maybe several somethings.

It hurt you. Traumatized you. You had no one to help you grieve, process—- so common. Now whether it was you that did something wrong or someone else that did it—- your heart is holding on to them/you and holding them accountable. As your soul remains stuck in the last, it is, in essence, stuck to the past; looking backward causes your soul to focus on that issue. Our focus begins to magnify the problem, seeking to prove that it's true.

BECAUSE WE CAN'T SEE what's in front of us, our mind and body also begin to get stuck—- not looking forward to the future with a clean slate but with clouded judgment. There is slime on the vision of souls.

NOW EVERYTHING that happens to us is interpreted through the lenses of "I am rejected, unworthy of a good thing."

THE BOTTLENECK OF YOUR LIFE might be the best-designed filter for your life. What has felt like a holding pattern has been your future, putting a demand to offload the past. The things that are preventing you from a forceful flow of good things HAVE to be removed.

THE LEVEL at which we forgive others or ourselves is the level at which we will be set free. Imagine if we could get to the point where we say:

"I FORGIVE YOU"

"I forgive you for hurting me."

"I forgive you for hurting me, and I release you."

"I forgive you for hurting me, I release you totally, and it will no longer be remembered in my heart"...

"I forgive you for hurting me, I release you totally, and it will no longer be remembered in my heart, and it will no longer prevent me from living my best life."

"I forgive you for hurting me, I release you totally, and it will no longer be remembered in my heart so it will no longer prevent me from living my best life, and I bless you and pray that you too may be healed from the circumstances that have caused you to do...."

I'VE DEVELOPED a habit that IS a filter. No one is exempt from things happening.

THIS IS a tool that I use nightly, if not in the moment itself.

Why?

There's no price tag I could put on living free from the hurts and opinions of other people. I wake up feeling weightless, happy, full of expectation and hope, ready to discover the day and what's in store for me.

People get in moods, and people are hurt. A future that depends on the mood or misfortunes of other people is VERY undependable.

EVEN MY OWN mistakes can't destroy the potential for more good things to happen in the future. As long as I don't take myself too seriously, forgive myself, and give myself grace and space to grow and learn.

I've created a checklist for you as a gift, to help you verbalize and release. You can grab it by clicking here.

Chapter 6

DISCHARGED

Prevention is better than cure is a well-known proverb that serves as a powerful reminder in our daily lives. It teaches us to live a healthy, disciplined, and stress-free lifestyle to avoid health problems or dis-eases. Moreover, it is simple to follow prevention methods to stay safe from any problem. Still, the cure is risky for our health because it does not guarantee complete wellness once we have suffered from certain ailments. Furthermore, it is far easier for us to prevent a problem from occurring than it is to solve one that has already occurred.

It's good to seek medical advice when we're sick, but it's even better when we don't have to seek any at all. Being healthy is preferable to becoming ill, which ideally is only possible if we use preventative measures and exercise caution. But what exactly does it mean to be healthy? It's more than just avoidance or absence of diseases. Most books say that to be healthy means to be in a complete state of physical, mental, and social health. However, these are just the end results of a healthy soul and spirit.

It is common for us to use the things that are seen to explain and understand the things that aren't. For example, we use the falling of an object to define the earth's gravity. With this knowledge, we can then deduce other unseen facts, for example, the force of gravity on the moon. Of course, it takes much more sophisticated testing and analysis, but you get the gist. So it is with the spirit - which is the highest expression of a man - and the soul. Whatever we see with our physical eyes is an expression of an unseen reality. This then means that things occur in the unseen before it is manifested in the seen. Secondly, while symptoms are an indication of a physical or mental dis-ease, these physical or mental dis-eases further indicate a disorder in the soul or spirit.

I wish I had known this a while ago when my memory was going to the pits, and I thought I was losing my mind. I knew memory loss was common for trauma survivors, but this was starting to scare me. I thought I had early-onset Alzheimer's, but I was even too young for that. The psychiatrist cried at our first meeting after hearing about my childhood. The Psychologist said my memory scores were below the tenth percentile. And the neurologist said the results showed that I had a tumor on my brain. This was real.

Different disturbances in the soul manifest themselves in different ways, just as different illnesses reveal various symptoms. Therefore, a differential diagnosis is important. In the medical world, a differential diagnosis is when we look at all things that are presented (symptoms) and differentiate which condition could cause it. This might require an interview, labs, and other tests and examinations. For example, many of my clients who suffer from suppressed anger and low self-worth also struggle with sinus issues. However, their reason for seeking me is usually a recent disruption at work or home. Anger is rarely mentioned – if they are aware of it, and declining self-worth is typically masked by false confidence. It is after the interview and examination that the root cause is revealed.

"Out of the abundance of the heart, the mouth speaks."

Because of our complexity, each person responds to events differently, if at all. Many people are still even unaware of these responses until they are manifested physically. It gets even more complicated since traumatic responses can occur from simply being bystanders. Ever wonder why you can't stand being in the presence of that person who has done absolutely nothing to you?

But how does one take preventative measures for their soul? I believe this verse says it best "Guard your heart with all diligence, for out of it are the issues of life." I used to miss the true meaning of this until I learned that the heart mentioned here is not my organ that pumps blood but rather the subconscious mind. This made it clear then that to guard it means to protect its gates which are our senses that communicate our external world. What we see, what we listen to, and the activities we engage in.

Are we watching things that breed love, gratitude, kindness, and joy, or are they rooted in fear, jealousy, anger, envy, and negative thoughts and feelings? Likewise, the things that we listen to. And what exactly are the thoughts that we are having and hearing? Are they always our own, or are they laced with otherwise negative suggestions?

To live a full life and the life you truly desire, it is important and necessary to be an active partaker and not just a passive bystander. This is especially true concerning your mind. After all, as a man thinketh in his heart (subconscious mind), so is he.

Though comparing the mind to a computer is a very simplistic view and is best reserved for metaphoric references, we shall use it here in an effort to keep things light. And just as you would protect your computer from harmful spam, viruses, and malware with the most recent McAffee security software, the same meticulousness should be employed for your thoughts. However, the same efforts and care are not applied to our minds. It is perhaps because we weren't taught how to.

I mean, as children, we were taught to listen and obey. To learn and to think in order to apply the things learned. What not to think and what to think. But not how to take control of them.

So the next time you see 'Lindsay,' and she doesn't smile at you, when the thought arises that she's not smiling at you because she doesn't like you, consider this:

1. Are those my thoughts, or are they some otherwise suggestions?

2. What is the purpose of this thought? Is it simply meant to occupy and

distract my mind, or is it a self-construct of a deeper self-sabotaging reason?

3. And finally, who gives a flying potato if she isn't smiling at you? In the grand scheme of things, why is it so important to you?

As mentioned earlier, as a man thinks in his heart, so is he. Some will see Lindsey without a smile and wonder if she's ok, while others will choose the example above. Your thoughts and words reveal what's in your heart. If you pay close attention, they will tell you.

Validating the thoughts that swirl around in our minds is crucial. This is the core of our soul's filtration system. When you are conscious of a thought, whether from internal or external sources, your validation of it is what determines how it is stored subconsciously, if any at all.

Let's use the case of Lindsey, for example. When the thought arose that she was not smiling because she dislikes me, I had two options: to either accept or reject it. The choice made here dictates the outcome. If I accept it, it gets downloaded in my subconscious as a fact, even if she was simply not smiling because her cat peed in her cereal. However, it doesn't stop there. This thought then becomes a belief that taints my perception of everything she does. You can see how easily this can spiral out of control.

Had I rejected the thought initially, it would've given me the opportunity to both check on Lindsey to see what's really up - perhaps I could've shared my cheerios with her – and it would also allow me to diagnose where that polluted thought arose from. Then I could address it and heal. This is how growth occurs.

Unfortunately, most people take the former approach, not because they are bad people, but simply because they are unaware or insensitive to their unseen symptoms.

My people perish for lack of knowledge.

Though this is a minor and arbitrary example, this is a constant process in our minds. Over time, if not managed, these negative suggestions and thoughts become a part of you, planted in the deepest part of our hearts. Then they begin to contaminate your relationships and everyone you interact with. Soon you become a shadow of your truest self, and the poison is indistinguishable. Years of negativity then lead to many more bad decisions, eventually leading to much regret in your life.

This can be hard and does take much practice, but the reward of a clean heart and peace of mind is so worth it.

Personally, I could not, in any way, shape or form, do this without the Lord Jesus Christ. I don't know your beliefs, nor am I trying to convince you in any way, but those who know me know. Since birth, I was always confident, positive, and triumphant regardless of the obstacle. But there came a point where I just broke. The more I triumphed, the more the obstacles...and they just kept increasing in intensity. I remember it so vividly. Sobbing in my living room, I said aloud, "God, if it wasn't a sin to kill myself, I would do it." I was so tired and over it. So, I continued on miserably until one day, I whispered at my bed, "God, who are you? Everyone has something different to say. So many different religions. Show me who you are." And show He did.

Ok, I know that you're thinking that this all sounds fine and dandy, but what happens when you take all the necessary precautions, but it still doesn't help. What happens when you take all the preventative measures but are still violated, and poison is forced within you? You didn't ask for it. You didn't desire it. But someone took it upon themselves to intoxicate you.

This is where I needed help. And fast. I'd intake too many poisons, and it had gotten fatal. It didn't matter if I was the victim. Poison doesn't ask questions before unleashing its effect. It was in me, and it had to go! My life depended on it.

Do not rejoice when your enemy falls,

And do not let your heart be glad when he stumbles. (24:17)

The term "enemy" literally means "hater" or "one who hates." This person has either harmed you in the past and has not repented or continues to harm you at every opportunity. The proverb warns against taking pleasure in that person's downfall, despite the temptation to see such misfortune as poetic justice. That desire, however, reveals a bitter and resentful heart that would exact its vengeance if given a chance.

We usurp God's role as the Supreme Judge of all people when we refuse to let go of resentment. By taking pleasure in our adversary's downfall, we accept calamity as justice. The focus then shifts away from the one who infringed upon our rights and instead shines on our now hardened hearts. In essence, we become our perpetrators.

Vengeance may be your daily grind. If that's the case, know that you're not alone in your struggle. However, it is a condition that affects the vast majority of people. There isn't a culture where vengeance hasn't left its mark—but that doesn't make it right!

Poison can be emotions as well as something you eat or drink. And one of them is hatred, which is a powerful emotion. This mental venom can pollute your spirit, poison your soul, and infiltrate all of your relationships. Anyone who has become entangled in the arms of hatred understands how damaging and mind-consuming it can be. Even the word has power, especially when spoken by a friend, family member, or child.

While hatred can be directed at almost anything - animals, foods, jobs, and movies - hatred towards other people is the most destructive.

In general, there are two types of hatred: the kind that is directed outward (explosion) and the kind that is directed inward (implosion). Both will eat you up on the inside, so if you find yourself living with hatred, today might be a good day to do some wellness housecleaning.

Personally, I refuse to give anyone the power to change me negatively.

Let your light so shine before men.

FIVE STAGES OF FORGIVENESS

1. Awareness

2. Anger

3. Allowance

4. Augmentation

5. Acceptance

Forgiveness is a topic that is frequently discussed without regard for the significance of the word. "You ought to forgive her." "You must forgive yourself." "It's fine; just be forgiving about everything." These statements look nice on paper, but the reality of forgiveness is much more complicated.

Forgiveness is a process, not an immediate result of a decision. You can't just say, "Oh, I forgive myself," and be done with it. Because forgiveness is all about letting go of emotion and accepting the outcome of mistakes, it requires effort and emotional understanding. It can be frustrating and depressing at times but in the end... It's worthwhile.

Learning to truly forgive can be broken down into a few steps. Let's just call them the five A's of forgiveness. Consider it in terms of the stages of grief. Before you can fully forgive someone, you must be able to move through each point, even if that someone is you. So, let's begin with the most basic.

1. **Awareness:**

Unlike its counterpart in the stages of grief, the first step toward forgiveness is the inverse: awareness. This step is all about checking in with yourself and determining your mental and emotional state. For example, consider the following if you have caused yourself or others pain: What effect has this had on you? Are you sorry for what you did? What impact have your actions had on others and/or on yourself?

This can be difficult and painful because we often avoid confronting our mistakes for fear of becoming depressed and anxious. On the other hand, looking away from the consequences of our actions causes us more depression and anxiety in the long run. In addition, it can lead to us repeating the same mistakes. Dive deep into your inner world of thought to discover how you truly feel about what you did. This requires complete honesty with yourself.

The process of harm inflicted on you by others is similar, albeit slightly altered. It is critical to understand how the harm has affected you. Examine your situation: How has this person affected you? What impact did their actions have on your happiness? What impact will these effects have on you?

Recognizing your pain is critical to understanding what it will take to forgive the other person and whether you even want to do so. Therefore, no matter how uncomfortable it is, it is critical to devote time to this step and ensure that you are willing to move forward with the forgiveness process.

It's perfectly fine if you aren't. Contrary to popular belief, forgiveness is not always immediate, but it is absolutely necessary. Even if someone directly apologizes to you, we sometimes need time and space before we're ready to welcome them back into our lives if we decide to do so. Allow yourself as much time and understanding as you require to complete this step.

2. Anger:

This step has two components. It starts with acknowledging the anger that has arisen during your awareness period. The rage is directed at the prospect of ever forgiving anyone, including yourself. You must be able to feel this emotion before you can accept it. But don't let yourself get caught up in it. Instead, find a way to reconnect with yourself after feeling whatever you need to feel. Perhaps find a friend who will let you vent to them or write a letter to the person who has hurt you (even if that person is yourself). You will not need to send the letter - It's simply releasing your emotions so you can let them go.

Allow your temper to cool before proceeding to the second part of this step. What else is there now that the rage has subsided? How will other emotions surface? What are your true feelings in response to what you or the other person did? Anger is frequently treated as the emotional source of our problems, but in reality, it is primarily used as a mask to conceal what we are truly feeling. Many complex emotions are buried beneath the initially consuming flashes of hatred. What are they like, and how can you get through them?

3. Allowance:

You can proceed to the "Allowances" stage now that you've released your anger and more difficult emotions toward yourself and others. Allowances, like "Bargaining" on the stages-of-grief scale, are all about acknowledging the why. Accept that there were reasons for the mistake you made or the other person's mistakes. Most things happen for a reason, whether or not that reason is directly related to the action taken. Internal turmoil, negative personality traits, and poor coping mechanisms can all explain, but not excuse, mistakes. It is critical to comprehend why someone did something. Only then can you move forward with accepting what they did.

4. Augmentation:

Take a long, deep breath. You're almost there. This step is about what you believe needs to happen in order for you to forgive yourself or the other person, as well as how you can move forward in the future. What caused you to make that error? What prompted the other person to inflict such harm on you? What can you and/or they do in the future to avoid causing further harm to either party?

Determine the steps you must take and explain them to yourself or the other person. Outline what steps you can take to begin limiting or encouraging certain behaviors in yourself. If they need to start treating you differently, work together to chart a course toward more positive interactions in the future.

5. Acceptance:

The final and fifth step. The most important and most difficult. Acceptance. This one is fairly self-explanatory. Accept whatever wrong you've done or what has been done to you, and then choose to forgive it.

You've determined the psychological impact of the harm. You've let go of the worst feelings associated with the harm. You've seen how you got here and have figured out how to get away from it. All that remains is to reestablish trust in yourself and with that person.

It will not always be simple. Forgiveness can be attained in these five steps, but, like grief, it is not always a straight line. Being hurt destroys trust and causes enormous emotional distress. It's about losing something you owned. Forgiveness is a means of regrowing what has withered away, but it is never a perfect or painless process. However, over time, it can alleviate pain and allow love to re-enter.

All you have to do is accept the path before you and take the first step down it.

Chapter 7

THE STORY

The toxic green witch may have stayed dormant within us for a long time, never realizing she was there until a situation or relationship revealed her existence. It's often in those places that the shame of the presence of the green witch makes us feel so ugly that we push away good people in an effort to preserve our self-esteem. We fight, run away, avoid, or emotionally disconnect from that person to avoid the condemning feelings of being "THE BAD GUY" - because absolutely no one wants to be the witch. At our core, we all want to be good, but when our ugly shows up in the mirror of our relationships, our natural tendencies are to do whatever we can to make that feeling go away, which may manifest itself a little differently for everyone.

Some blame; if it's someone else, then it's not me.

Some avoid/disconnect; if I stay apathetic, then I don't have to feel anything.

Some fight others; if I overpower them and hurt them first, they can't hurt me.

Some run away; If I leave this situation, the problem won't exist.

All of these defense mechanisms are temporary relief from the symptoms of pain yet never solve the real problem. And so the issue remains and repeats, over and over, even throughout generations, unless someone becomes humble enough to see it and brave enough to uproot it.

The break-up or dissolution of the relationship was probably chalked up to "just not good together," "toxic relationship," "Irreconcilable differences," "we fight too much," or something along those lines.

Sadly, if an action by someone who is good to us is perceived as similar to an action from someone who'd previously hurt us, and that wound hasn't been properly tended to, our response from our unhealed emotion and nervous system will be the same as though we were facing the same threat.

If we lived in a bubble alone, for example, we might feel confident about our "abilities" as people, about the condition of our hearts. The presence of another, as they respond to the unlovely behaviors we express, serves as a mirror and reveals the invisible wounds of our souls. I'm not sure about you, but seeing "ugly" come out of us isn't fun; it can feel humiliating and shameful. If the person on the other end is secure enough in themselves to not take your wounds personally, you may feel safe enough to live with those wounds and let them heal. But if two wounded people are constantly wounding each other more, their hearts remain guarded and ignorant of the roots of emotional pain.

Many couples in marital turmoil have said, "I'm better off single" because it's much more "comfortable" to live ignorant of our own failings. Ignorance is bliss, right? It just doesn't serve us well in healing and growth. It's easier to divorce ourselves from any situation that would force us to peel back the layers and deal with the unforgiveness in our hearts.

Unforgiveness is an emotional and mental state caused by a delayed response to forgiving an offender. Everyone has been hurt by the words or actions of another. Perhaps your best friend forgot your birthday, your father criticized your career path, you were bullied as a child, or your spouse had an affair. Someone who was molested as a child may find it difficult to forgive; people who have been raped may find it difficult to forgive themselves and those who assaulted them, and children who were neglected by their parents or guardians may find it difficult to forgive. It hurts to be wronged, whether the offense is serious or minor.

We've all felt the sickening pain in the pit of our stomachs when we've been mistreated, especially by someone we care about. This pain can leave emotional wounds of rejection, fear, betrayal, and insecurity; instead of choosing forgiveness, unforgiving people drink the poison of unforgiveness; that is, they drink poison expecting someone else to die; that is what unforgiveness does to people who bear the burden of unforgiveness. Unforgiving people find it difficult to forgive; they carry the baggage of unforgiveness with them for the rest of their lives; many unforgiving people find it difficult to let go of wrongs that happened or happened to them many days, months, or years ago. Unforgiveness binds people to the burden of carrying unneeded baggage of unforgiveness.

Unforgiveness can be your way of hurting yourself when you are hurt. You've made yourself the judge, and you've decided on the punishment that the wrong-doer deserves. You feel justified as you burn with rage while telling your story to a friend or rehashing the offense alone. Every thought or word is a piercing dagger aimed at the person who has wronged you.

You can punish the offender with a cold attitude or distance, or you can hurt back with threats, ridicule, accusations, and criticism. Unforgiving people believe that debt was created when they were wronged, and as a result, an expectation of payment arises. People in this area are at risk of developing a self-righteous attitude and a sense of entitlement. You begin to believe that the world owes you something. Because you now have something to hold over the offender's head, the debt elevates you to a "superior" position. In other words, you can use the error to control and overpower the perpetrator.

When people are hurt, they feel vulnerable and powerless. Fear is at the heart of unforgiveness. Most people fear being hurt again, so they harden their hearts to avoid the pain. In preparation for another attack, the wounded begin to construct walls around their hearts. You may think to yourself, "I will not be duped into thinking this person is nice again, so I am dismissing them." "I will not be trodden on again."

Using unforgiveness for retaliation, power, weaponry, and protection may make you feel stronger and more in control, but these so-called "benefits" are only a mirage. Accepting unforgiveness will only result in incarceration because you allow the offender to control you. As a result, you may experience loneliness, which can have a negative impact on your social and physical well-being.

Moving forward and experiencing healing from previous hurts and pain requires forgiveness. This is often difficult to achieve, but it is possible through a slow process in which we cognitively and emotionally forgive only to have positive memories. When people do not forgive and experience symptoms of sadness, depression, or anxiety, serotonin levels in the brain fall below normal, leading to other problems such as obsessive thinking. Because obsessive thinking is rarely a relaxing activity, it can result in increased levels of stress hormones (cortisol) being released into our bodies.

Being hurt by someone, especially someone you love and trust, can elicit feelings of rage, sadness, and bewilderment. Grudges filled with resentment, vengeance, and hostility can take root if you dwell on painful events or situations. If you allow negative feelings to overpower positive feelings, you may become engulfed by your own bitterness or sense of injustice. Some people are more forgiving by nature than others. Even if you hold a grudge, almost everyone can learn to be more forgiving.

In the movie the Matrix, the Character Neo was offered a red pill or a blue pill. The red pill represents the willingness to learn a potentially unsettling or life-changing truth, and the blue pill means he would remain content in ignorance, never discovering what life would become if he took the leap. The red pill would give a complete understanding of everything that was transpiring in Neo's life and also guidance and direction towards the next steps in his life.

Now you all have a choice. This is where you have the ability to choose the red pill or the blue pill for your own life.

The red pill is an example of what life would be like if you were able to identify and forgive the people who wronged you, abused you, and took advantage of you; the situation that has kept you stuck in the same place would unlock your shame, hurt, PTSD, and anger.

This would give you extreme clarity and allow you to discover your true potential, and give you a way forward.

The blue pill is staying stuck in the same cycle; no one wants that, and I don't want that for you.

The red pill/blue pill is a metaphor; the deeper meaning of this is walking in wholeness, completely healed of the trauma you went through because you came into the power of forgiveness. It may seem hard right now because it feels like a weight you have been carrying for a long time.

That was never meant to be. Someone stole from you your innocence, the power of forgiveness resets you back to the original manuscript, and you can internally return to your innocence.

This is why I have shared my stories with you. I was verbally abused, rejected by my family, raped multiple times, and beaten by society because I was labeled a victim.

I was stigmatized in my surroundings, trying to find things to satisfy me, from sex to alcohol, and moving to different countries, looking for different places to change what happened to me. Happiness is not in the next place, the next job, or the next partner. But happiness is not where you are; rather, true happiness comes from within you.

One day everything clicked for me; it wasn't the satisfaction of the things outwardly that would give me short-term happiness; it was dealing with the roots that were created by the trauma.

I was able to deal with each root and pluck it out by forgiving the individual who had hurt me. It wasn't easy, and it did take time, but in a season of rediscovery, I was able to go through each person, each event, one by one, and forgive them.

It was the greatest moment of my life.

The blindness scales came off when I was able to power my way through forgiving every single person and not holding them in contempt any longer. The person in contempt was "Me."

Detox means a process of time in which one abstains from or rids the body of toxic or unhealthy substances; detoxification.

This is where your soul detoxification process begins. Where you free yourself from the anger, the hurt, the memories, and we run the toxins of unforgiveness from your being.

This process will become the adventure you get clarification, substance, and delivered from the enemy that has kept you hostage, which is, Unforgiveness.

If you feel you cannot do it alone, I will walk you through helping you discover your true purpose, living life again in zeal, finding out who you were born to be, detoxing from the events, and living in the power of forgiveness. Click here for support.

Chapter 8

FORGIVENESS FOR DIFFERENT POISONS

When we talk about a filtration system, generally, it removes the toxins and containments from anything we attach to it. Anything that has a certain amount of toxins in it will not be able to function properly and will eventually run out in the longer run.

Anger, frustration, fear, and other "negative emotions" are all natural human emotions. They can all cause stress and are frequently viewed as emotions to be avoided, ignored, or otherwise bypassed, but they can also be beneficial to experience. There are several reasons why managing them without denying them is a better approach.

The concept of "managing" negative emotions is complicated. It does not imply avoiding them—avoidance coping is a type of coping that attempts to do so, and it frequently backfires. It also does not imply allowing these negative emotions to wreak havoc on your life, relationships, or stress levels. If we allow it, unmanaged anger, for example, can compel us to destroy relationships.

Managing negative emotions entails accepting that we are experiencing them, determining why we are experiencing them, and allowing ourselves to receive the messages they are sending us before we release them and move on.

Yes, that may seem strange, but our emotions are definitely designed to be messengers to tell us something. If we pay attention, these messages can be extremely valuable and provide us with some life – lessons. Negative emotions must be managed so that they do not overwhelm us. We can control them without denying that we are feeling them.

When we discuss so-called negative emotions, it's important to remember that these emotions aren't negative in the sense of "bad." They are more in the realm of negativity than they are of positivity.

Emotions are neither good nor bad; they are simply states and signals that allow us to pay more attention to the events that cause them. This can motivate us to create more or less of a particular experience. For example, negative emotions, unlike some others, are not always pleasant to experience. But, like most emotions, they exist for a reason and can be quite beneficial to experience.

You may believe that a disease or illness is to blame for your tired body or prolonged aches, but have you ever considered that negative thinking could be to blame? Pessimism has an impact on more than just your emotional health. Doctors have discovered that people who are negative are more likely to suffer from degenerative brain diseases, cardiovascular problems, and digestive issues and recover from illness much slower than those who are positive.

Negativity is frequently the result of depression or insecurity. It can be caused by illness, life events, personality issues, or substance abuse. Negativity, like many other things in life, can become a habit. Criticism, cynicism, and denial can all create neural pathways in the brain that promote sadness. These negative tendencies can cause our brains to distort the truth, making breaking the negative cycle even more difficult. Fortunately, most habits can be broken.

Negative thoughts and emotions are a natural reaction to tragedy and heartbreak. However, prolonged bouts of negativity can lead to serious health issues. Negativity triggers our bodies' stress response or 'fight-or-flight' mode. Our bodies are programmed to respond to stressful situations by releasing cortisol into the bloodstream, which increases alertness and focus. While some stress is beneficial to our health, excessive stress can be harmful. Negative emotions slow digestion and reduce the immune system's ability to fight inflammation. This is also why pessimists are more likely to get sick than optimists.

We first need to understand the difference between getting hurt and getting harmed in order to understand the way to healing and moving on. We often become enraged when we are insulted, disrespected, ignored, or treated in an uncivil manner. That anger can linger in us for weeks, then grow so large that it disturbs us on the inside. It is at this point that some people consider forgiving those who have such power over them.

If we first ask ourselves, "Have I been harmed by what happened?" we may not need to take the step of forgiveness. Harm is defined here as something concrete in this world, something tangible, something that not only hurts on the inside but is also destructive on the outside.

- A punch to the face that bruises or breaks a bone is considered harmful.

- A ruined reputation that makes it difficult to find a good job is harmful.

- Arresting someone on false charges is harmful.

- Having one's feelings hurt without any physical contact is an offense, but it does not necessarily result in harm.

- Being told in private to work harder, which deeply embarrasses but does not jeopardize one's job, is an offense, not harm.

- Being falsely accused by someone with no legal authority and no consequences is an offense, not harm.

We must sometimes distinguish between being offended and being harmed. That is exactly what the legal profession does. According to the lawyers, we do not have a legal right not to be offended by others.

When we distinguish between offense and harm, we can calm our inner rage because we realize: The person hurt my feelings but did absolutely no actual harm to me. Is it really necessary for me to carry this kind of inner burden?

Who is suffering as a result of my carrying all of this around, the person who made the insensitive remark or me? The answer may assist the questioner in letting go of the issue and moving on without carrying the resentment, which, if deep and lasting enough, may lead to a lack of confidence and even anxiety or psychological depression.

At the same time, people can fall into inner traps in which the offense itself causes so much inner turmoil that forgiveness is an essential step in emotional release and regaining emotional health. Not all offenses that are recognized as non-harmful can be easily dismissed, so the option of forgiveness must be available. However, for many people, simply stepping back from the inner dialogue and realizing that no harm was done can be healing. Moving on and forgiving are two very different things. One can move on by putting the situation behind them and not harboring resentment toward the person who offended them. To forgive is to make an effort to be good to those who are not good to the offender.

So, have you been offended by anyone? What specific harm has been done to you? Are you able to proceed if there are none? If not, perhaps forgiveness is in order. If you have been harmed, forgiveness may be just what you need to get your emotional life back on track.

After going through all this, you get to learn a lesson for sure. It's true when they say that everyone comes with a lesson in our lives. It all depends on us how we take it. Life is a rollercoaster ride full of both good and bad experiences, with good experiences providing immense happiness and bad experiences providing lifelong learning. Tough times teach us valuable lessons for our future.

Humans are social animals who make mistakes in their lives. These mistakes are painful at the time, but they become important lessons later on in life. Tough times bring out the real person in us, teach us the difference between right and wrong, and determine which friends and relatives will be with us in the long run. In a nutshell, a bad experience helps a person become a better person.

Although misfortune brings with it a lot of learning, this does not mean that we should wait until we are in a bad situation to learn the lesson, even though there are lessons to be learned from the difficulties of others. Because smoking is harmful to health and causes cancer, we should not try to learn about its dangers. There are numerous other examples from which we can learn a lifelong lesson, such as alcohol, drugs, reckless driving, crimes, and so on.

Some traumatic experiences can alter a person's life. So, instead of waiting for the worst to happen, learn from the lives of others and, when it happens to you, fight with the mindset that it is only temporary and will teach you a valuable lesson in the end. So I agree that a difficult time is a valuable learning experience for everyone. This is exactly how we should take bad experiences. A negative experience should teach us a lesson, and when we are done learning, we should forgive and move on, which is the only way to healing.

Every act of forgiveness has great worth. You can forgive yourself, others, and even yourself when you don't know who to forgive because forgiveness isn't about who is to blame or who is at fault. It is about completely and permanently letting go.

Forgiveness is acknowledging that what happened has already occurred and that there is no point in allowing it to dominate the rest of your life. Forgiveness clears the slate and allows you to move forward.

Are you planning on exacting vengeance? That's just negative thinking getting the best of you. There is, however, a positive way to seek vengeance. How? Leave them alone. Remember me. Working on becoming a better version of yourself is more fulfilling than clinging to the contempt of others. Allow it all to go and focus on your growth and kindness instead. Suppose you train yourself to be more loving in your thoughts and actions on a consistent basis. In that case, your positive energy will attract more positive results into your current reality.

Be the polar opposite of the person or situation that hurt you. Allow yourself to let go and grow beyond your pain. Continue to live well in a way that brings you peace of mind. The energy you would expend attempting to exact true vengeance would be better spent creating an amazing future for yourself.

Happiness is the best revenge because nothing drives your adversaries insane more than seeing a new smile on your face.

To help you forgive in different circumstances, the following list can help you understand how to deal with these situations.

1. **Forgiveness for unkind words:**

It is relevant and valid, regardless of how you feel after saying unkind words. Accept and validate your hurt, whether it was intentional or not. Engaging in a hurtful exchange will not solve anything; instead, it will make matters worse. Instead, journal, talk to a friend, or do something productive until you feel more at ease.

2. **Forgiving your children or younger family members:**

Nobody does family perfectly. We sometimes say and do things that hurt the feelings of our loved ones. We are all guilty of "sins" of commission or omission toward those we love. Forgiveness is an important component of strong, healthy relationships.

Forgiveness is the ability to free one's mind and heart from all past hurts and failures, as well as feelings of guilt and loss. Forgiveness allows us to overcome anger, resentment, and the desire to punish or exact revenge on someone who has wronged us. Forgiving entails altering your thoughts, feelings, and behaviors toward the offender. Bad feelings and judgment toward the offender are reduced, not because they don't "deserve" it, but because we view the offender with compassion, benevolence, and love.

When couples and families fail to forgive, unequal relationships form and persist. True closeness is impossible because the "offended" holds the "offender" in bondage, and the victim's obsession with being wronged and seeking vengeance also holds the victim in bondage. The person who made the error or harmed the other is kept in a "one down" position, indebted to the other.

According to forgiveness researchers, family members from all families must humbly seek and grant forgiveness for their relationships to survive.

3. **Forgiveness for infidelity:**

Make reconciliation optional, but forgiveness mandatory. People frequently go about it backward, preferring to reconcile rather than forgive. This traps them in the agony of betrayal, preventing them from moving on to a new life. Don't reconcile if your friend is in danger. Don't put any pressure on yourself to decide on reconciliation during the first year of recovery. It could take up to a year to determine whether it is safe to reconcile. Reconciliation is contingent on your mate's ongoing recovery as well as your ability to recover from the trauma of the betrayal.

4. **Forgiveness for neglect or abandonment:**

Describing abandonment and the associated thoughts, feelings, and reactions necessitates more than a simple definition of the term itself. The antidote to forgiveness is the medicine required to heal the soul from abandonment. Forgiveness is frequently misunderstood; it does not simply forget what someone else has done to you. Forgiveness does not imply forgetting or absolving someone of responsibility for what they have done to you. Forgiveness is something that you give to yourself.

5. **Forgiveness when there is a suicide:**

Forgiveness is a process that evolves over time rather than something that happens overnight. It is about coming to terms with the loss as well as the manner in which the loss occurred. Suicide loss is a particularly heartbreaking experience. Suicide raises many questions about why people commit suicide. Unfortunately, the clarity of the reason is lost with the person, so there is always that question mark. So it's about getting used to the ambiguity of that question never being clearly answered. Once you're more at ease with it, it could be one of the first steps toward forgiveness.

So much is often called into question for the bereaved person, including their loved one's love for them. This is an expected part of the grieving process. Because anger is a natural part of grief. Suicide attempts and completions frequently result in distorted thinking. Many people, for example, come to believe that ending their own life is an act of kindness to their family, as if they are harming their family by remaining alive. You'll never know what your mother was thinking, but the context for this act is her life and relationship with you.

6. Forgiveness when there is a murder:

Forgiving a murderer does not bring back the person who was killed, but it does allow you to let go of your anger and hatred, and it does help you see the world in a different light. It's about letting go of the things that keep you from living a happy and fulfilling life.

7. Forgiveness in the case of rape:

Despite conflicts such as insecurities, confusion, and fear caused by flashbacks and trauma inflicted on victims, there is hope for recovery, healing, and possibly forgiveness. It does necessitate a significant amount of processing and time. It requires consultation with psychiatrists and therapists. Of course, it's not easy.

The larger issue for rape victims is not forgiveness but self-recovery in order to be fully functional participants and meaningful producers/givers of society and its needs.

Chapter 9

ANTAGONISTS OF FORGIVENESS

Before we dive into this chapter, I want to take a moment to clarify the difference between perception and reality. Yes, it is necessary for us to discuss because we could save ourselves and others a world of hurt by this simple distinction.

We've chatted about offense and harm, and how the things we validate consciously shape 'our reality.' This reality that we create is called our perception. It is the ability to become aware of something through our senses. This is great, but this is also where many problems lie.

Let's say, for example, you met someone and they gave you their phone number but instead of saving their name as Jim you accidentally put Kim. Now when your phone rings you think that it's Kim calling instead of Jim.

Okay, not the best example, but you see where I'm going with this. If someone is walking around with unhealed trauma, and many are, then the likelihood of misperception is increased.

And we see this all the time.

Someone was verbally abused somewhere along the road so now that they're having a conversation with someone who culturally speaks loudly, they misinterpret it as anger or insult...and respond accordingly.

Someone has been deceived by friends or colleagues so now when they see a gathering talking and laughing, they think it's about them...and respond accordingly.

Someone has had an unfaithful partner so when they see their current partner on the phone at night, they think they're cheating (though they're on the phone with their sibling)...and respond accordingly.

And from there, if there isn't great communication, things easily spiral out of control leading to separation, vengeful acts, and even death.

Consider an example of war. Some people believe that war is sometimes necessary to achieve and maintain peace. Others believe that war is evil and should never be entered, no matter what. Who is correct? Is war good or bad? What you see as accurate is only defined by your belief structure. Your version of what is real is only your perception of it, not what is necessarily true.

Let's take another example: suppose an event occurs in your life. You have a choice in how you react to it. Assume there is a death in the family. You can choose to see that event as terrible and tragic and then respond accordingly. You can also see that event as something that inspires you to do more with your life, to live each day as if it were the last.

You can see from that example that you may or may not have control over the events in your life, but you can certainly control how you respond to them. That aspect of life is always within your control. This is where life becomes interesting because your beliefs shape your reality.

Your belief structure influences your perception, influencing how you respond to events. Following that sequence, you can see that there is another place to begin. You have the option of examining your beliefs and then changing them. That is why I believe that everything begins with a decision.

Skewed perceptions

It's important to remember that how you choose to perceive things determines how they appear to you.

Now let's talk about antagonist and the role it plays in general, as well as in forgiveness. In literature, an antagonist is typically a character or group of characters who oppose the story's main character, the protagonist. An antagonist, such as the government, can also be a force or institution with which the protagonist must contend.

In medical science, we define an antagonist as a substance that blocks and acts as a barrier and performs the opposite function of an agonist. It binds to receptors and prevents them from producing the desired response.

In layman's terms, there is what is called a lock and key mechanism. Some cells in our body have proteins called receptors aka the lock. This is what many drugs and substances are created to react with. An agonist is something that causes the cell to perform its function, aka the key. An antagonist is a substance or drug that blocks the cell from functioning. Think of the antagonist as someone stuffing gum in a keyhole.

There is nothing special about an antagonist. Its sole purpose is the block the keyhole so that when you try to insert the key, it won't work.

Let's take a moment to talk about when I accidentally cut my finger with a butter knife. Okay, I'll take a moment and wait until you're done giggling.

Now my thumb is bleeding like crazy. The nerves started to send a ton of messages to my brain that "hey bud, we have an injury. Send out the immune system troops." My pain receptors are now activated and my thumb is throbbing.

I remembered I had some Advil and take 2 and they work their way to the receptors and start to block the keyhole so that pain receptors are activated less and I start to get some relief.

I also rubbed my finger a lot so that the sensation of my touch could compete with the pain messengers, thereby decreasing the awareness of the pain. This is totally unrelated to our point, but I thought I'd add it because it's cool. So the next time you kiss someone's boo boo, you are in fact kissing their pain away.

Coming back to the reason why we have discussed all these medical terminologies and concepts.

Forgiveness is essential for our well-being physically, psychologically, and spiritually. Sometimes, we must forgive people even if we don't want to. That's because forgiving them is better for us, not for them.

However, things such as pride, hate, jealousy, and greed can serve as an antagonist to forgiveness and block our soul keyhole (insert smirk).

These antagonists will act as a barrier and will not let us forgive the people we should. This is why self-reflection and honesty are imperative to your healing so that you can identify the source of hurts and resistance.

I find many people struggle in this arena. So I created a program called Life in the "F" Lane and also why I am writing this book. So that you can have all the tools you need to kick trauma and pain to the curb and live the life of awesomeness that you were created for!

Chapter 10

EXTRAS

No one plans for horrible things to happen to them. Even despite many of us growing up in incredibly dysfunctional homes, as children, we spend hours rehearsing in our imaginations and at play the wonderful life we expect to have as adults.

With a cape tied around our necks, we jump from one couch to the other, chasing down the bad guy.

We will be brave and heroic.

In our bedrooms, we adorn ourselves in our mother's jewelry and sneak into her lipstick.

We will be beautiful and worthy.

All we need is another friend or sibling, and we play house as we take turns holding the baby dolls.

We will be nurturing and loving.

Our lego towers become intricate and more complex, finger paintings cover the kitchen tables, and play-dough figures get ground into the carpet.

We will create amazing things.

All those dreams we had seemed to live on the inside of us as we came into the world with them.

Somewhere along the way, a dream crusher, innocence stealer, hope robber, or identity twister came and served us something we didn't want and certainly never asked for.

Without permission and without notice.

I certainly didn't expect life to serve me up such a cruel night at 13 years old; on the very first day, I got to socialize outside of the four walls of my bedroom. Until the end of that night, I was confident that the tide of my entire childhood was changing. But it wasn't, it didn't, and it got worse. Way worse.

Instead of being embraced, comforted, and put into therapy, I was punished. Stone-cold was rejected and then labeled "the bad kid."

I know you wouldn't be here if something horrible didn't happen to you. Something you didn't ask for and certainly didn't deserve.

You know you didn't deserve it, right?

You Didn't Deserve this!

I wouldn't have to say this if I hadn't already seen this toxic lie survive in the heads of abuse victims, but you didn't deserve any of the bad things that happened to you at the hands of someone who couldn't control themselves.

"I wouldn't have hit you if you hadn't made me so mad."

"You wouldn't have gotten raped if you weren't dressed like that."

"I wouldn't have yelled at you if you'd just acted more like your brother."

"I wouldn't have beat you up if you hadn't been flirting with that guy."

"I wouldn't have if...."

Phrases like this are an abuser's way of blaming their victim and revealing an expression of guilt for what they did without taking responsibility for it.

The truth is no one inherently deserves abuse. We are each accountable for how we act and treat others, which is probably why you're here in the first place. You've probably noticed anger and irritation triggering you, causing you to treat another person in ways you feel badly about.

And that's exactly what's different about you. You've pressed into the pain and made a step towards fixing it.

Before we go on, please allow me the honor to tell you what you did deserve, what you were born worthy of having.

Just because you understand that those who hurt you were also hurting (which is true) doesn't mean you still deserved bad and weren't worthy of good.

You deserved a family that loved you, listened to you, understood you...believed IN you.

You deserved parents that kept their hearts open and loving to you, even when you did terrible things or failed.

You deserved parents who taught you things about life: cooking, cleaning, budgeting, relationships, spirituality, LOVE... you deserved a guide, not to figure it out all on your own.

You deserved a home; a warm bed, clean clothes, food to eat, and a bath.

You deserved innocence, the choice to be intimate with a person you loved, not forced, and not forced to use the most vulnerable parts of your body as a form of currency.

You deserve to have peace, safety, comfort, protection, and love in your own home.

You deserve warmth, kindness, and patience; utter adoration and delight when you walk into a room.

You deserve truth, loyalty, and honor.

ALSO BY AUTHOR

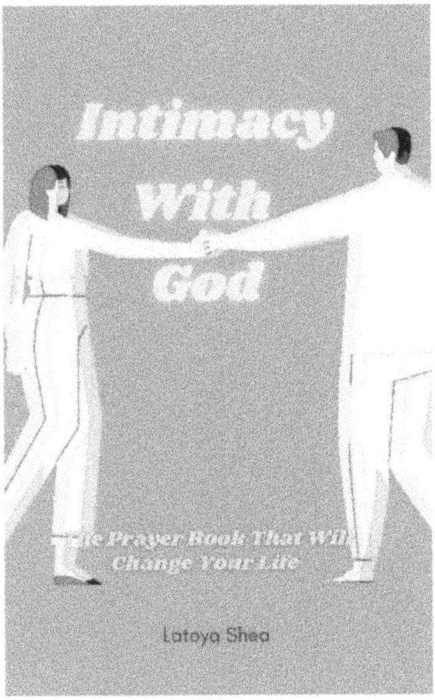

#1 Bestselling Book

www.ingramcontent.com/pod-product-compliance
Lightning Source LLC
LaVergne TN
LVHW011337080426
835513LV00006B/411
* 9 7 9 8 9 8 6 9 7 7 0 1 0 *